PHOTOS, FOOTPRINTS
AND FLASH

Jerry R. Rosen

Photos, Footprints and Flash

© 2025 Jerry R. Rosen

Purple Works Press
41 Avenida Fernando Luis Ribas
#449
Utuado, Puerto Rico 00641
www.purpleworkspress.com

ISBN: eBook 979-8-218-85479-9
ISBN: Paperback 979-8-218-85480-5

Printed in the USA

Dedication

I am deeply grateful to my best friend, life partner, and wife, Maxine, as well as to my entire family for their love and support, which made the writing and publication of this book possible.

Table of Contents

Chapter 1: The View from The Middle

Brian Miller came into the world as a middle child, born on Wednesday, March 15, 2000. As an adult, when asked about his birthday, he often joked that he was "born in the middle." When pressed, *the middle of what?* He'd grin and rattle off his reasons: it was the middle of the week, around noon, sandwiched between his older brother Peter and younger sister Amy, and between two historic moments, Y2K, when 1999 rolled into 2000, and September 11, 2001, the day America was struck by an attack that claimed over three thousand lives. For good measure, he'd add that it was also the infamous Ides of March.

Some who heard this curious explanation would ask why he knew such detailed trivia about his birth and whether it meant anything to him. True to his nature, Brian remained silent and let people guess the answer to that question.

Brian was the son of Harold and Ellen Miller, who lived in a modest four-bedroom mid-century home located in a middle-class Brooklyn neighborhood. The house had been passed down to them after Harold's father, George, died a few years into Harold and Ellen's marriage, well before they began having children. Until then, they'd rented a mid-rise apartment in Queens.

Before George died of a heart attack, he had already lost his wife, Betty, to a combination of illnesses that had plagued her for several years. Both George and Betty were only children, as were Harold and Ellen. As a result, Peter, Brian, and Amy grew up with no grandparents, aunts, uncles, or cousins. Brian often found himself wondering what it might have been like to be part of a larger family.

When Brian was just a year old, his older brother Peter died from Sudden Infant Death Syndrome (SIDS) shortly after turning two. The loss shrank the already small family. Harold and Ellen were grief-stricken when they were told there was nothing they could have done to prevent the loss of their child at such a young age. The tragedy became a life-altering moment for both parents. In their grief, they poured their love into Brian, devoting themselves to his well-being and ensuring he grew up healthy, happy, and deeply loved. Two years after Brian's birth, his sister Amy arrived, completing their family of four.

Harold Miller, who had never attended college, owned and operated a small but financially successful shoe store in Brooklyn. Ellen, on the other hand, had earned a degree in education and initially pursued a career in teaching. However, she soon found the job overwhelming and emotionally taxing. She quit teaching after only a few short years, just before Amy was born. She chose to become a stay-at-home mom until Brian and Amy were old enough to care for themselves. This decision was made for two reasons: the family couldn't afford independent childcare, and neither Harold nor Ellen felt comfortable leaving their young children in the care of strangers.

As Brian and Amy grew from infants and toddlers into school-age children, they made friends easily. They also went through periods when they fought with each other, as siblings do, but their bond deepened whenever either felt threatened by someone else, whether a child or an adult. They experienced the instinctive and natural dynamic that comes with sibling rivalry, and their relationship grew closer in the years that followed, extending into their adulthood.

During the years Brian and Amy attended elementary and middle school, Harold and Ellen spent their Saturdays with them, going to local movie theaters. After the films, the family would enjoy dinner together at nearby, inexpensive restaurants in Brooklyn. As Brian and Amy grew older, their outings began to take them farther from home—boarding the subway and traveling into Manhattan, where Brian and Amy were exposed to the "Big Apple." Amy remained less intrigued by the city, but Brian kept extensive notes in a diary about the various Manhattan neighborhoods, fueling his growing sense of adventure. Later in his life, this information actually became very helpful to him.

While in high school, Brian started taking the subway into Manhattan on his own or with a friend in an effort to learn as much as possible about the culture and vibe of the city, from the Lower East Side to Broadway, Wall Street, and even Central Park. He thrived on what he was learning during each venture and felt that someday he would want to leave Brooklyn and live in "the City," much like Frank Sinatra, who had admitted to staring toward New York City from New Jersey, dreaming of doing the same thing and making it there.

One of Brian's closest companions during this time was Michael Freedman, or "Mike" as Brian called him, his best friend since childhood. Mike was the only child of a well-off family who, despite their financial advantage in their community, remained warm, welcoming, and well-liked by their neighbors and friends. Brian felt comfortable visiting the Freedmans' home despite the fact that it was much newer and significantly larger than his parents'. This, in turn, helped foster a bond between Brian and Mike that lasted through high school, into their college years, and later in life.

Growing up, Brian was somewhat interested in baseball at first, but during his high school years, he became fonder of basketball. As a high school sophomore, he made the varsity basketball team as a point guard, maintained decent grades, and was more socially involved with friends than his sister. Amy was far more interested in her grades and maintained a competitive edge over Brian in that department, believing she needed to stand out in something different. Amy had absolutely no interest in sports during the time she was in school, turning instead to drama class and taking part in plays, while Brian developed a more serious interest in sports—and in girls. But there was never any doubt in either Brian's or Amy's mind that if push came to shove, they would be best friends, always.

Brian had tried to learn more about his brother, Peter, but all of his baby photos and belongings had been discarded. No two families deal with the death of a child in the same way. While it was Ellen's decision, more than Harold's, to remove everything related to Peter from their home, Brian always felt he had missed out on a chance to connect more with his family and secretly blamed his father because, even when he asked directly, Harold would avoid the subject. This eventually left some holes in their relationships later in life for Brian, Amy, and their parents. Amy dealt with it by making as many friends as possible in school and later in her life in an attempt to fill that missing piece in their family tree. Brian kept his own feelings about Peter to himself, but in his heart, he felt that emptiness.

As Brian grew older, he chose to remain in Brooklyn, rarely strayed far from the greater New York City area, and stayed close to home. He joined his family on a couple of vacations in other parts of the country but never strayed far from where he grew up. After graduating from high school, Brian chose to pursue a degree in Arts & Sciences at The City College of New York. He did so for a few reasons: The school was affordable; it was easy to reach using public transportation, allowing him to continue living at home and commuting; and it offered an academic path he wanted to pursue—journalism or something else that would provide both stimulation and a decent way to make a living. Mike's family could afford to send him to a more expensive college, and he chose Columbia University, a private Ivy League school where he earned degrees in business and law. The fact that Brian and Mike were the same age but separated by what their families could afford did not affect their friendship in any way. They remained close through their respective college years and later in life.

Amy also attended and graduated from The City College of New York, likely because Brian chose the School of Arts & Sciences, and she had some understanding of what he was studying, so she decided to follow in his footsteps. However, journalism was not a path that interested her. Shortly after graduating, she felt a bit lost and decided to find a job while she figured things out for herself. She found work in a major Manhattan department store. What was meant to be a short-term plan turned into a much longer stay. It offered her a place to go each weekday, to interact with people, and to get paid while thinking about her future.

While Brian and Amy were in college, Harold continued to own and operate his shoe store. Ellen, however, decided she needed greater personal stimulation and began working in a nearby floral shop. The pay she received helped cover bills at home, but more than that, she enjoyed creating beautiful floral arrangements for her customers.

While Brian was still attending college, he felt he needed to create a plan to move out of the family's modest four-bedroom home after graduation in order to gain additional freedom and move forward with his life. Amy, however, chose to continue living with her parents after completing college. The Miller home then gained another occupant, a small black-and-white border collie named Flash. He was named Flash by Harold because of his ability to change direction in a flash, much like a herding dog.

During his high school and college years, Brian continued to contemplate a future as a journalist, but he soon began to realize he was passionate about all forms of creative expression, from paintings to photography. During this mental journey, he had the opportunity to see the works of renowned photographer Ansel Adams, which stood out as a very different approach to photography. The black-and-white photos Adams captured drew Brian's attention. As he continued taking classes in college and exploring as many forms of art and design as he could, he found himself gravitating more toward photography and becoming less enthusiastic about pursuing journalism.

By the time Brian graduated from college, he knew he needed to create a plan to make enough money to move out of his family's home and gain the privacy he preferred. Because of the costs associated with renting an apartment large enough for a living space, a bedroom, and a darkroom where he could develop his own film, he began looking for part-time jobs.

Like most people who live in the greater New York area, Brian was willing to use public transportation to avoid the high cost of owning and maintaining a car. He kept the bike he'd had since high school and decided that making the most of the city's buses and its famous subway system was all he needed to enable him to work as a messenger by day and a bartender by night. That was the plan he hatched, and it soon became a reality.

Chapter 2: Across The Frame

A few years had passed since Brian graduated from college, and now, at 25, he was pursuing a career in professional photography while living in New York City and working side jobs to pay for his rent, food, and other essential expenses.

After searching for a suitable place to live for nearly six months, Brian finally hit a home run. He had been looking for a place to move out of his family's home. Most apartments were either on high floors without elevators, in areas where the noise from nearby traffic and late-night garbage pickups was disruptive, or came with a host of other issues, not least of which was their cost. Mike called Brian to let him know he had a friend who was aware of a small, quiet Manhattan apartment that might be a perfect match. This place was owned by someone both Mike and Brian knew and trusted but hadn't initially considered contacting. The size was just right, and the rent was surprisingly affordable. The building was small, with only studios and one-bedroom apartments; there were no children and just a few pets. It was perfect.

So, that piece of Brian's plan fell into place, and with a few furniture items from his bedroom at home, his clothes, and other personal belongings, he was able to move in quickly and without much expense, turning what he considered his dream apartment into his new home.

The apartment had a small kitchenette, which was not a problem for Brian since he mostly ate frozen food that he heated up in the microwave. As a bonus, there was enough room for him to keep his bike safely indoors and in good working order year-round. There was also a strange little storage closet without a window, which was perfect for his darkroom. All of this fell into place as if a script had been written and a floor plan had been drawn up just for him.

At this point, Brian was working as a messenger during the day and bartending at night. The location of his new apartment was perfect, much closer to both his jobs, and he felt his prayers for that part of his life had been answered. What he needed now was to get more serious about what he really wanted to do with his time: pursue photography in a more creative way.

Good professional film cameras were becoming scarce as everything went digital, making it difficult for Brian to find the camera he wanted. He finally turned to shop in pawn shops until one day, he found an older camera in better-than-good condition, which had been sold by someone who couldn't find a traditional buyer. Once again, Brian's prayers had been answered.

Brian began experimenting with his newly found camera and soon realized he would need a plan to balance his time—to work and to pursue photography, both in daylight and at night, in different seasons and under different weather conditions. Brian was used to being outside as a messenger during the day and indoors at night as a bartender, but it was not easy to align his days off from both jobs. He really needed the income he was earning, which meant he had to solve this scheduling challenge in a way that would enable him to pursue his passion.

It took Brian several months to figure out a schedule that let him work as a messenger and a bartender while also dedicating more serious time to his camera. This required him to change messenger companies twice and find a bar that offered enough flexibility for him to take an entire day off, both during the day and at night, to explore New York City in search of something worth shooting.

During this time, he was also able to improve his camera skills, learning to use shutter speed and aperture to achieve the kind of photos that met his expectations. What he hadn't yet figured out was which subject matter he wanted to focus on, people, places, or things.

Chapter 3: No Hard Feelings

When Brian was working as a messenger, he was always rushing through traffic, focused entirely on staying safe, delivering packages quickly, and making sure nothing got damaged. As a bartender, he had to shift his mindset to becoming more relaxed and learning to be a better listener to his customers. He quickly learned that the less he talked and the more he listened, often just nodding his head, the better his tips were.

Brian was now a messenger by day, moving at full speed; a bartender by night, honing the skill of listening; and on his days off, he found himself wondering why he carried a camera in his backpack.

All of this kept him busy, but little by little, Brian began meeting people his age: friends from college he met through Mike, and others from his two jobs. He grew close to a few guys he felt he could trust and started going out with them, if for no other reason than to stay socially connected.

Brian's default personality was that of an introvert. That didn't hinder his messenger work and wasn't a serious obstacle behind the bar either. But the truth was, he was starting to feel lonely.

Some of the parties he began attending weren't just guys watching sports and drinking beer. More and more, he found himself at parties where women were part of the scene. This wasn't something he had ever really given much thought to, but when he began meeting women his age who seemed interested in what he did—both for a living and what was, at that time, only a hobby—he became interested in them too.

Brian continued to widen his circle of friends he had met while at college and, in turn, some of their friends. This new chapter gave him a broader understanding of the dating scene in New York, something he hadn't really been interested in until now.

As his circle of friends grew, so did the variety of people he was meeting. Some had been born in New York and came from middle-class families like his. But he also began to meet people who had moved to the city, either with their families or alone, to chase the Big Apple experience. This latter group had significantly more money than Brian, and he found it hard to keep up with their taste in restaurants and nightlife.

At one party, hosted by a friend of Mike's, Brian was pouring himself a drink when a woman beside him offered a shy smile.

"You always look this serious or is it the punch?" she asked.

He chuckled. "I think it's the playlist."

She laughed. "Fair enough. I'm Rebecca Gordon, by the way but you can call me Becky."

"Brian."

They clinked glasses.

"So, what do you do?" she asked, leaning against the kitchen counter.

"Messenger by day. Bartender by night. And in between... photographer. Kind of," he added.

Her eyes brightened. "What kind of photos?"

"Mostly street stuff. Candid moments. New York when it forgets it's being watched."

"That's poetic," she said.

"Occupational hazard."

Becky smiled. "Why street photography?"

"I think because the city's always moving. It's chaotic, messy, but every now and then, it gives you something... a look... a shadow..."

"That sounds like something a writer would say, not a messenger."

He grinned. "Aha, I think it's the same chaos but different lens."

She took a sip of her drink and seemed to be studying him. "Do you ever show your work anywhere?"

"Not really. Just my wall and a couple of folders on my laptop. Sometimes I think about it, though."

"You should," she said. "I'd like to see them."

Brian blinked. He was caught off guard by the simplicity of her interest. "Yeah? You mean that?"

"Sure. People want to see the world through someone else's eyes. Especially someone who actually *sees* things."

He looked down at his cup, then back at her. "You always this thoughtful with strangers?"

She winked and said, "Only when they don't make me regret it."

He laughed. "Guess I'll try not to mess that up."

"You're doing fine so far."

There was a beat of silence between them, but it wasn't awkward. Becky glanced toward the hallway.

"You want to step out for some air?" she asked. "This place is getting a little warm."

Brian nodded. "Definitely."

After that party, Brian lay down on his bed and recalled the affairs of the night. He actually felt good just being himself around Becky. He learned that she worked as an executive assistant at a New York legal office. She was quiet, kind, and a good listener. She seemed genuinely intrigued by Brian's goal of becoming a full-time professional photographer, even if it meant juggling two part-time jobs to reach that dream.

They started seeing each other two or three times a week, mostly going to nightclubs that catered to a younger crowd in Manhattan. Becky lived with a roommate in Queens, so if they wanted privacy, it usually meant heading to Brian's apartment after leaving the club.

Brian's routine was becoming just that, a routine: working two jobs, trying to find interesting places to take photos on his only day off, and spending time with Becky. He began to feel like he was just going through the motions. Becky was nice to be with, but she lacked something he couldn't quite put his finger on, something that would make him want to take the relationship further. That uncertainty started to nag at him. Small things Becky did, or didn't do, began to annoy him.

Unbeknownst to him, Becky was having similar thoughts. She liked Brian, trusted him, and there was nothing specific she disliked. But still, she wondered: what about my future?

One evening, they went out to dinner. It was a quiet little Thai place Becky had picked. They sat across from each other in a booth, flipping through the menus without saying much.

After they ordered, the conversation stayed light. A bit about work. A weird customer Brian had at the bar. Something about Becky's roommate leaving dishes in the sink. It all felt... fine. But only fine. Beneath the surface, they both had their own thoughts about their relationship.

Brian poked at his rice with his fork. Becky was quiet, looking like she wanted to say something but wasn't sure how to start.

"So, Mike's throwing a thing on Saturday," Brian said. "You wanna come, or...?"

Becky hesitated. "I might have something with Amanda. Not sure yet."

"Cool, no worries."

She took a sip of water, then smiled politely. "What about you? Are you still taking photos on Sundays?"

"Trying to. Last weekend I just walked around and didn't shoot anything. Couldn't get in the mood, I guess."

"Maybe you're overthinking it."

"Yeah, maybe."

Neither felt an urge to discuss it, until the conversation drifted in that direction.

"I was talking to my mom yesterday," Becky said, tracing the edge of her plate with her finger. "She asked if you were coming home with me for Thanksgiving."

"Oh." Brian gave a small laugh. "What'd you say?"

"I said we hadn't talked about it."

He nodded, then looked at her. "Have we... talked about anything like that?"

"Umm, actually no. Not really." She smiled faintly. "I think we've kind of been... cruising."

"Yeah." He exhaled softly. "That's exactly what it feels like."

It was awkward at first, but then, almost simultaneously, they both leaned back in their chairs.

"I like you, Brian. I really do," Becky said. "But maybe we're better as friends."

"Yeah. Same here," he said, almost relieved. "So... no hard feelings, right?"

"None."

They smiled, and just like that, it was settled. There was no big drama. It was an amicable breakup that gave Brian an unexpected sense of relief that surprised him. After dinner, they went their separate ways, back to their own apartments, and they never saw each other again.

Brian had reached the conclusion that it was time to stop dating Becky and return to being what he was: a messenger, a bartender, and a photographer.

Chapter 4: A Call That Changed Everything

Just when Brian thought he had his life pretty much figured out, aside from deciding where to go on his days off to take photos, his life took a dramatic turn.

Brian was halfway through a delivery run, rushing through traffic, when his phone buzzed in his pocket. He pulled over and was clearly annoyed, until he saw the caller ID. It was *Amy*.

"Hey, what's up?"

"Brian, stop what you're doing. You need to get to the hospital. Right now."

"What?" His stomach dropped. "Wait, what hospital? What happened?"

"Maimonides Medical Center. It's… it's Mom and Dad. There was an accident."

Brian froze. "An accident? Are they—how bad is it?"

"I don't know all the details yet," Amy said, almost crying. "They just said it was serious and there have been major injuries. That's all I know."

"I'm on a run," he muttered. "I… I just have to drop this off."

"Brian, please!" She was crying now. "I'm already here. I'm alone. I don't know anything."

"I'll be there in ten minutes. Just hang on."

Brian completed his messenger run as quickly as possible, then headed straight to the hospital. When he arrived at the emergency room, he learned that both of his parents had indeed been in an accident. He found Amy waiting for him, distraught and in tears.

Brian wasn't as close to his parents as some sons might be, but they did see each other at least once or twice a month. He saw his father as someone who had always made sure the family was provided for, even with the modest income from running the shoe store.

At that moment, Brian was actually more concerned about how his sister was holding up, since she still didn't know any of the details about what had happened. So, all they could do was sit together and wait.

After about thirty minutes of nervously waiting for news about their parents, the nurse in charge of the emergency room approached Brian and Amy to explain what had happened.

"Brian and Amy Miller?" the nurse asked.

They both stood up at once.

"I'm Julia, the charge nurse," she said. "I have some information from the ER team. The police were able to speak briefly with your father before he lost consciousness."

Amy's eyes widened. "He was awake?"

"For a short time, yes," the nurse replied gently. "He told the officers that he and your mother had been out shopping for a piece of furniture, I believe for the living room. They didn't find what they wanted, so they were heading home."

Brian glanced sideways at Amy, then back at the nurse. "What happened?"

"On their way back, while going through an intersection… a truck ran a red light and struck the driver's side of the car. It hit them full-force."

Amy covered her mouth with her hands. Brian stared straight ahead.

"I'm very sorry," the nurse said in a low, sympathetic voice.

This was no movie, and when the medical staff told them what had happened, it came as a major blow to both Brian and Amy. A few minutes later, the senior attending physician came out to speak with Brian and Amy.

"I'm Dr. Patel," he said. "I'm the senior attending tonight. I was with the trauma team when your parents were brought in."

Brian stood a little straighter. "How are they?"

"I'll be honest with you both. Your mother sustained catastrophic injuries in the crash. She passed instantly at the scene. There was nothing we could do."

Amy let out a sound, somewhere between a gasp and a sob, and backed into the wall, sliding down onto the nearest chair.

"No, no, no..." she whispered. "She was just shopping. She was just..."

Dr. Patel gave her a moment, then continued.

"Your father is in critical condition. He has multiple injuries, including significant head trauma. He's in a coma."

"Is he going to wake up?" Brian asked, almost unable to speak.

"We don't know yet," the doctor said. "There's concern about internal bleeding in the brain. We're running tests now. Surgery is not an option at this time. Right now, we're keeping him ventilated and stable with fluids. That's all we can do."

Amy's eyes brimmed with tears. "So, we just... wait?"

"Yes," Dr. Patel said. "I'm sorry. I truly wish I had better news."

"Can we see him?" Brian asked.

"We'll let you know as soon as he's been moved to intensive care.

It'll be soon."

The doctor gave them both a moment of quiet before nodding again and walking away.

Brian slowly sat down next to Amy, who was still crying into her hands. He reached over and gave her a side hug, wrapping his arm around her entire body. Amy broke down completely and couldn't stop sobbing, clutching Brian as tightly as she could, trying to absorb and make sense of the news.

Then, even worse news came fairly quickly. Brian's father would also lose his battle before the hospital staff could do anything more to save his life. Within an hour of the accident and being rushed to the hospital, both Ellen and Harold were gone.

The sudden, traumatic nature of the situation hit like a brick through a window. It all happened so fast, and then it was over.

After only a few moments trying and adjust to the shock, Amy turned to Brian.

"Brian... you're going to have to handle this."

He blinked. "Handle what?"

"All of it. The arrangements. The calls. The—" she paused, swallowing hard, "funeral stuff. Whatever needs doing."

It was the kind of situation the family had never even discussed.

Brian had stopped hearing things even before Amy suggested he needed to take control. His vision was blurred, and everything felt distant. He had never contemplated having to deal with the sudden loss of either parent, and now he was in uncharted territory.

He turned back to Amy and tried to offer a few moments of comfort. Then, he approached the first nurse he could find and asked if there was someone at the hospital in a clergy position he and Amy could speak to. There was.

Brian and Amy were ushered into a small chapel, and shortly afterward, a hospital clergyman named Richard arrived. He represented a religion that didn't matter to Brian at the time. Richard approached them gently and asked how he could help.

Brian and Amy had grown up in a home largely devoid of religion. The family observed major holidays, but they were never affiliated with Christianity or any other formal faith. They simply took the days off when Easter and Christmas came around, sometimes spending them together, sometimes doing their own thing or celebrating with friends.

When Brian and Amy were younger, they had asked questions about faith and what their parents believed. They were essentially told that if, someday, they felt inclined to explore a more structured religious path, that would be completely fine with both parents.

Brian told Richard what had just happened and asked for two favors. First, he asked Richard to say a prayer for his parents while he and Amy held hands. Richard complied with a quiet and solemn nondenominational prayer for Harold and Ellen. Then Brian asked if Richard could refer them to a funeral home to help with the arrangements that would need to be made. Richard did as requested and also gave Brian his business card, suggesting they keep it and call if they had any further questions or needs. Brian shook his hand and thanked him. He was still lost in a fog of his own.

When Brian and Amy returned home, Brian took the lead. He told Amy that he would figure out what options they had and that everything was going to be alright.

In just under two hours, Brian had transformed from a part-time employee working two jobs with an important hobby that was supposed to lead to a career into someone taking charge of a situation he had never faced before. He did it as if he'd been doing it all his life. He was running on adrenaline, but he also knew that someone had to take charge. Both their parents were gone, and his sister was inconsolably in shock, unable to function.

Chapter 5: The Business of Grief

The next day, Brian began working through everything that needed to be done. He was still in shock but refused to let himself grieve. Something deep in his mind kept telling him to keep moving until there was nothing left to handle. For now, he knew he had to stay completely focused on the present.

Brian quit both his messenger and bartender jobs after explaining to his employers that he had too much to manage regarding his parents' estate. He told them he hoped they would understand and welcome him back when he was able to return.

Mike suggested that Brian hire a local estate attorney, Stephen Ross, who Mike knew personally. Brian took his advice and engaged Ross's law firm to assist with the probate process that now had to be navigated. This led to several surprises revealed to both Brian and Amy during their meetings with Stephen.

Although Brian's father had supported the family, albeit on a modest income from his shoe store, he had purchased a life insurance policy large enough to allow Ellen (and their children, if necessary) to maintain the same lifestyle in his absence. Harold and Ellen had also created wills leaving everything they owned to each other, and, in the event of a dual catastrophe, to Brian and Amy in equal shares. This included all cash in their bank accounts, their mortgage-free family home, and all other assets.

There was enough money available to purchase burial plots at a nearby cemetery and to cover all arrangements required by the state, along with additional items, including headstones, now being recommended by the funeral director they were working with.

Brian and Amy were both shocked to learn that their parents, particularly their father, had put all of this in place without ever mentioning it to either of them. However, there were no instructions regarding what to do with the shoe store.

Brian decided to personally reach out to the owner of the building where the store was located to try to negotiate a way out of the lease so the store could be closed and the merchandise sold to wholesalers. The landlord, who had been close to Harold, agreed to help and was willing to terminate the lease without penalty to Brian and Amy.

Brian's first trip to the store to inspect the furniture, fixtures, equipment, and inventory, something he recalled from a business class he once took in college, came with a few surprises. He had never spent much time at the store and didn't really know how it was run. In a small office at the back, he found the store's bank checking account records (with a small but reasonable cash balance), some outstanding invoices, and additional accounting books, including previous bank statements. All of this had been stored in a safe that didn't lock. There was nothing else of value inside.

Then, while looking behind the front counter near the cash register, Brian discovered a small cigar box tucked under the counter. When he opened it, he couldn't believe his eyes. There was approximately $2,500 in cash inside. There were no notes, entries in the books, or records anywhere to explain the cash. Brian took the money for safekeeping and decided to tell Amy later, before informing anyone else of what he had found.

Brian and Amy held a meeting to discuss what to do with the house and with Flash. A next-door neighbor had been coming into the home to make sure Flash was getting food and water and was taking him for walks while Brian and Amy dealt with the many other details. That same neighbor suggested they contact a local real estate agent he knew, who could help determine the market value of the home and assist them in deciding whether to sell it. This would depend on whether they wanted to sell, or if Amy chose to stay, and Brian wanted to move back as well.

That conversation had already taken place between them. Neither wanted to live there anymore. They did not want to deal with the memories, the upkeep, or anything else associated with the home. They would need help selling or donating the contents, assisting Amy in relocating to a place she liked and could afford, and then getting the house on the market. They agreed to split the net proceeds evenly, in the spirit of what their parents would have wanted.

This was unfamiliar territory for both Brian and Amy, so they relied on the real estate agent and their attorney, Stephen Ross, who had already been helping with the estate. Stephen explained the probate process, the order in which things needed to be done, and referred them to other resources to handle the home's contents. Although they were required to follow New York state probate laws, the wills Harold and Ellen had prepared made the process smoother than it might have been otherwise.

When the subject of Flash came up, Amy admitted she wasn't sure how to take care of a dog.

"I don't really know what to do with him," said Amy, watching Flash as he circled and lay down near the door. "I've never taken care of a dog on my own."

Brian nodded. "Yeah, I figured. That's why I've been thinking… maybe I should take him."

Amy looked over. "You would?"

"If you're okay with it," he said. "My building allows dogs, and I think he'd be alright there. It might take time, but I can build a routine with him."

Amy hesitated. "He's been following me around a lot lately. I think he's still looking for them."

"I know," said Brian. "But he's starting to come around to me, too. Yesterday, he sat by my feet for almost an hour while I was sorting through boxes."

"That's something," Amy said softly. "He always loved Dad. I think he's still confused."

"Me too," Brian said. He reached down and rubbed Flash behind the ears. "But I'll take good care of him."

Amy gave a short nod. "Okay. That sounds right."

Time seemed to move at two different speeds for Brian. Some things happened very quickly, while others would take more time. He knew that holding a funeral for his parents had to be the highest priority, even as discussions about the house and the store were already underway. Many decisions still had to be made, and Brian wanted Amy to be a full partner in the process. However, Amy asked Brian to simply keep her informed while she tried to manage her emotions and adjust to the changes she now faced.

Amy had friends living as roommates in a home on Long Island and reached out to ask if there was room for one more. When they learned of her situation, they immediately welcomed her to join them.

Brian shifted his focus back to the funeral home, contacting family friends and others he believed would want to attend the service. A couple of days had passed since the accident. The children thought it was time to lay their parents to rest.

Brian had been moving quickly, multitasking, and getting very little sleep. He completed the arrangements with the funeral home. Two days later, a graveside service was held, followed by a reception at the Miller residence for those who wished to pay their respects. That part was over.

Stephen guided Brian and Amy regarding the bills that needed to be paid following the funeral. The home was cleaned out by an estate company and then prepared for sale. Amy had moved to Long Island as planned. Brian also decided to move forward using some of the money he and Amy received to buy a vehicle for himself and Flash. There was space to park near his apartment, and he felt this was one of the changes he needed to make. Getting around on a bicycle for the rest of his life was probably not a great idea. He also knew the family car had been totaled and was no longer available if he needed it.

The home sold quickly after it was listed, bringing additional cash to both Brian and Amy. Brian chose to buy something small but practical for himself and Flash. That turned out to be a black Jeep Wrangler, which seemed perfect for his needs. It was not very expensive, would be easy to park anywhere in the New York area, and could handle the winter weather.

Brian also found a few companies to purchase the merchandise, furniture, fixtures, and equipment from the shoe store. With Stephen Ross's help, he worked out the lease termination, so the shoe store was now also off Brian's list of things to address.

He spent a quiet evening with Flash at his side after all of this was behind him and reflected how people with no prior experience or knowledge would ever know how to handle what he and Amy had gone through. He pulled a bottle of beer from the refrigerator and stood for a moment before twisting off the cap.

He raised it in a small, private toast. "To Mom and Dad," he said quietly, and then sat down on the couch. At first, he just stared ahead, trying to process the past few days. Then the silence got to him, and the weight of it all broke through. The tears came without warning. He didn't try to stop them. Flash climbed onto his lap and remained there, waiting for Brian to get up, but Brian could not move for hours. It was the first time he had let go of his emotions.

Around midnight, he wiped his face, looked down at Flash, and said softly, "We're a team now."

Then he stood up, walked into the bedroom, and lay down. Flash jumped up beside him. They both fell asleep almost immediately.

The next day, Brian contacted Mike and asked for a meeting at Mike's law office with Amy present. One more issue needed to be clarified. Brian and Amy asked Mike whether the company that owned the truck should be sued for damages, including compensation for the pain and suffering caused by the truck driver's negligence. Brian and Amy had always known this topic would need to be addressed, but neither of them wanted to face it. They set it aside until they had completed everything else on the checklist for closing the estate. Now, that time had come.

"You're right to ask. It's a complicated process, and it can take time," Mike said, leaning back in his chair and folding his hands.

Amy looked at Brian, then back at Mike. "We're not even sure how something like this works. Would you be the one to handle it? Or does this need someone else?"

Mike shook his head. "Honestly, I wouldn't be the right person for this kind of case. You're talking about a wrongful death suit involving a commercial trucking company. That requires a litigator, someone who's used to dealing with big insurance carriers and legal teams."

Brian frowned. "So, what do we do?"

"I can refer you to someone," Mike said. "Andrew Forman. He's handled several high-profile cases like this. Knows what he's doing, and he's aggressive when he needs to be."

Amy leaned forward. "Would we need to pay him up front?"

"No," Mike said. "It's usually a contingency fee. He only gets paid if you win or settle. I can set up a meeting for you two to talk to him, go over the details, and see what you think."

Brian glanced at Amy. "That sounds okay?"

She nodded. "Yeah. Let's meet him. We don't want to drag this out."

"I'll call his office this afternoon," Mike said. "You'll be in good hands."

A few days later, Brian and Amy met with Andrew Forman. He had significant experience suing and winning lawsuits against trucking companies in situations similar to the one that caused the death of Harold and Ellen Miller. They discussed the standard contingency fee structure and other details Brian and Amy would need to understand before deciding whether to proceed.

During the meeting, Brian and Amy turned to each other and agreed there was no reason to wait. They signed a letter of engagement with Andrew and instructed him to file the lawsuit and keep them informed throughout the process.

Brian was also rethinking whether he really wanted to return to work as a messenger and bartender. Both jobs, along with his pursuit of photography, had been put on hold. The funds he and Amy had received after all the estate's debts were settled would give him more time to focus on what he truly wanted—to become a good enough photographer to sell his work and restart his life.

His parents' accident and sudden death had taken a toll on him, but he didn't want that tragedy to derail his plans of becoming a professional photographer. Brian had faced their deaths head-on and taken care of everything. He notified the messaging company and bar owner that he would not be returning. It was time to move on.

Chapter 6: Cadence of the Days

It took time for Brian to feel comfortable settling into a routine as a photographer and nothing else. He knew he had done everything possible to put the past behind him, but he also realized that if he didn't get his dream of becoming a professional photographer back on track soon, he might lose all the momentum he had worked so hard to build—momentum that had been so abruptly interrupted.

Brian also came to understand that his new best friend was Flash, and that's where he needed to start. Flash's life had been upended along with Brian's and Amy's when the only people he truly knew disappeared, forcing him to move to a place he'd never been. Despite Brian's best efforts to grow closer to him, it was clear that nothing resembling a truly close bond had yet developed.

With that in mind, Brian decided to put together a mini travel pack for Flash and take him along on every trip, even if it was just to the corner store. They needed to start doing everything together so Flash could become familiar with Brian's schedule, personality, moods, and habits.

Having the Jeep made it easier to get away to new places, away from the city, giving Flash the chance to break free from being just a neighborhood pet and instead become a true partner to Brian. They began taking longer trips and embarking on new adventures into wooded areas and parks around New York. Brian picked a different location every day, determined to make this their new normal.

Communication between Brian and Flash also became a priority. Brian worked on teaching Flash to understand and follow basic commands, even for something as simple as getting ready for a walk or a ride.

"Alright, buddy," he said, rubbing the dog's ears. "We've got some work to do, you and me."

Flash tilted his head. His ears were twitching, as if he was trying to understand.

"From now on, you're not just a pet. You're my partner. Partners stick together, right?" Brian smiled. "So, that means you come with me everywhere. Trips, shoots, even coffee runs. Sound good?"

Flash wagged his tail cautiously. His brown eyes were focused on Brian.

"Okay, first things first." Brian held up a hand. "Sit."

Flash blinked, then sat down slowly, unsure.

"Good boy! See? You're a fast learner." Brian stood and grabbed his keys. "Now let's practice. Walk or ride?" He jingled the keys.

Flash barked once and trotted toward the door, tail wagging faster now.

"Ride it is." Brian chuckled. "You're gonna love the Jeep. But listen, Flash, this isn't just about getting out of the house." His voice softened as he opened the door. "It's about me and you and building trust. We're a team now. You watch my back, and I'll watch yours."

Flash gave a little huff and nudged Brian's hand with his nose.

"Yeah, I know," Brian said with a grin. "You're ready. Let's hit the road, partner."

Brian saw this as an opportunity to get some time away from what he had just been through and to share the experience with someone else. Flash was now a friend and a partner, and this would help them bond more deeply and quickly.

***

After a month of Brian and Flash following the same routine each morning and evening at Brian's apartment and venturing somewhere different during the day, a new pattern began to take shape for Flash. Brian felt it was starting to pay off. Flash began to anticipate what Brian would do next, which was critical for Brian's mental health and survival moving forward.

Brian then expanded what he and Flash did each day to include serious photo scouting, just as he had in the past, this time bringing Flash along. He was curious to see how well Flash would understand what he was doing, walking quietly through a wooded area, stopping, aiming his camera, and taking photos—while giving only soft commands for Flash to walk, stop, and sit before continuing. This new routine was meant to teach Flash to stay calmly under control in case they came across wildlife that Brian didn't want to startle. But Flash, being a border collie, might have had other ideas, and that wouldn't be helpful.

With each passing day, Brian realized Flash was even smarter than he'd expected and was proving to be an intuitive learner in his new environment. Training him to follow commands turned out to be easier and quicker than Brian had expected, something he wasn't sure about when he first began working with his new partner. Flash had never received this kind of training from Harold or Ellen in his previous life. But if they could work as a team, Flash would get the exercise he needed, stay sharp, and become a much closer partner to Brian than he had ever been to anyone before.

As Brian and Flash continued exploring new places together, Brian also found an opportunity to unwind and enjoy nature in a way he never had in his own past. No longer working as a messenger or bartender and instead focusing on training his senses to lead him to subjects for photography, he found it was helping him heal as well.

Adding to this new life, the change in seasons and being outdoors, away from city life, brought a new awareness to Brian in terms of his photo subjects as well. He had been taking pictures of people in the city, but now he saw trees and wildlife, which actually felt more peaceful. The tranquility of not having a set schedule during the day gave him more freedom to concentrate on things he might not have even noticed a year or two ago. By connecting his brain to his other senses, it seemed as if an entirely new world was opening up to Brian. He fully realized what was happening and embraced it.

Thus, Brian and Flash had accomplished a magical transformation into a new world together, brought about by the tragedy in their lives. They were finding new ways to work better and grow closer to each other, while Brian began discovering photo subjects that now attracted him, subjects he otherwise never would have noticed. Everything began to come together again for Brian, or maybe for the first time, really. All of his senses were working, and he was feeling joy, perhaps for the first time in his life.

As a bonus, Brian's focus changed when it came to taking photographs. He realized that even a black-and-white photograph of a bench or a tree could become art if he made the right adjustments with his camera, depending on the time of day or the lighting on his subject. Each night, after spending the day taking pictures, he found new excitement in developing his film and discovering whether what he remembered photographing had actually resulted in something he, or anyone, could relate to as art. Some photos he had to reject immediately, making note of the mistakes he had made so he wouldn't repeat them.

Brian continued with this approach each and every day. He began to understand what worked and what didn't, which allowed him to do a better job in the field when hunting for new subjects for his portfolio. The adjustments Brian had made, combined with living alongside Flash, meant his new approach to life was going to work!

Chapter 7: A Little Family, After All

During the time Brian and Flash were creating new lives together as partners, Amy was also going through some changes, although much less dramatic and much slower.

Amy was still living in a four-bedroom home located in a small community on Long Island. On occasion, one of her roommates moved out, but they were quickly replaced, as demand for rental housing in this community was high. Amy's arrangement was that she rented a bedroom but shared the rest of the home, including two bathrooms and a kitchen, with her roommates. Everyone Amy came into contact with where she now lived was either attending college or had already graduated, and all had part- or full-time employment in or near Manhattan. Despite occasional changes in roommates, there was a sense of commonality among the four women, and that brought a relative calm for Amy, which was something she knew she needed.

Brian and Amy had made a pact to stay in touch on a regular basis so they wouldn't just drift apart. They both expressed a fear that could happen and agreed to text each other at least once a day and try to get together once a week as well. As the weeks and months passed, even Flash warmed up to Amy, recognizing she was a special friend to Brian and a safe human to know. Over time, Flash and Amy became closer, but not as close as Brian and Flash were when they were alone or working together each day.

On one occasion, when Brian, Amy, and Flash were together at Brian's apartment, Flash did something he had never done before. Brian and Amy were sitting side by side on the floor of the small living room with their backs against the couch and legs stretched out in front of them. They were talking softly about their routines and how everything was going.

Across the room, Flash moved from his little bed, gave a quick shake, and trotted over. Without hesitation, he wedged himself right between them, half of him curling into Amy's lap and the other half pressing his head gently into Brian's legs.

Their conversation stopped instantly. Amy and Brian both looked down, surprised, then at each other, and without saying a word, they understood. What Flash had just done mattered. It was his way of choosing, connecting and claiming them.

"Did he just...?" Amy began.

Brian gave a small laugh. "Yeah. I think he just joined the conversation."

"He gets it," Amy murmured, running her hand slowly over his back.

Brian nodded, resting his palm on Flash's head. "Yeah. He knows we're his people now."

Amy smiled. "This is the first time he's done this."

Flash gave a small, contented sigh, then leaned into them with the weight of someone settling in for good. They laughed together, reaching down at the same time to hug him. Then, with perfect timing, he lifted his head and gave each of them a messy, wet kiss—first Amy, then Brian—before flopping back down.

"I guess that's that," Brian said softly. "We're in this together now."

Amy smiled and glanced at him. "The three of us… a little family."

There was a bond in that moment that remained, helping them both realize that family means different things to different people. Animal lovers would understand this. At that moment, Brian, Amy, and Flash became equal parts of a big bowl of love.

On occasion, Brian had to attend appointments where pets weren't permitted and needed a place for Flash to stay for the day. He wasn't sure how long he would be gone and didn't want to leave Flash alone in his apartment all day. Amy had no problem taking time off from work to stay home and pet-sit Flash. More importantly, Flash seemed just fine being alone with Amy.

When Amy stayed with Flash, she walked him on a leash through her neighborhood, giving them both a better opportunity to bond and allowing Flash to see and smell new things in a place far from Brian's apartment. He had no issues adapting to new routines, and that helped create an even closer bond—something that, as it would turn out later in their lives, would become important.

Chapter 8: Autumn Brought Her

Approximately a year and a half after the passing of Brian's parents, and after forging a close bond with Flash, Brian decided to return to the city for outings in one of his favorite places to escape: Central Park. As a bonus, this park offered easy access for both Brian and Flash in a familiar location.

Brian wanted to explore as much of the park as possible—on different days, in varying weather conditions, and throughout the changing seasons. The park offered many attractions and opportunities for a photographer: artificial lakes, waterfalls, meadows, woodlands, and the Central Park Zoo. This spectacular park was renowned for its picturesque beauty, with lush green landscapes and breathtaking views in almost every direction.

To Brian, it quickly became their new playground. It would be nearly impossible to grow bored. The better Brian came to know the park, the more intentionally he could plan his outings tailored to the season, in hopes of capturing a fresh perspective each time he went hunting for new photo material with his secondhand camera, still loaded with black-and-white film.

Spending time in the park almost every day brought about the inevitable: he and Flash began seeing familiar faces. People jogging, biking, picnicking, or enjoying lunch on a bench slowly became part of the park's rhythm, and part of theirs.

On one occasion, Brian was walking Flash on his leash across a wide grassy area. He was studying the trees that had already shed their leaves. It was autumn, and many of the trees stood completely bare. Brian paused, carefully aimed his lens at one particular tree, and snapped a few photos.

Only then did he notice someone standing quietly behind him, trying not to disturb his focus. Flash sat patiently in his "sit and stay" position with his eyes on Brian, awaiting the next command.

Brian turned to greet the young woman who had been watching him, but she spoke first.

"I'm sorry," she said quickly. Her voice was soft but clear. "I didn't mean to disturb you."

"You didn't," Brian replied with an easy smile. "Really. I'm Brian and this is Flash, my partner and best friend."

She smiled back, though there was a flicker of hesitation behind it. Her eyes moved from Brian to Flash, then to the tree beside him, and then back to his face. Her smile deepened, touched now with curiosity.

"Hi, I'm Heather Parker," she said. "May I ask you a personal question?"

"Of course," Brian responded. "Ask me anything."

Heather took a couple of steps forward to get just a bit closer and asked, "Of all things, why are you interested in taking a picture of a tree in the fall with no leaves on it?"

Brian chuckled slightly before responding. "Why not? Must a tree have leaves to have beauty? Besides," he added, "I'm using black-and-white film."

"What?" Heather exclaimed. "Who does that?"

"I do," Brian replied, laughing. He then gestured toward a nearby bench. "Would you like to sit for a few minutes? I can tell you more about the tree, the black-and-white film... all of it."

Heather hesitated, then smiled. "Sure, why not? I'm intrigued."

As they started walking, Flash, without a word from Brian, rose and padded toward Heather. His eyes were stayed fixed on her. He was alert but calm, watching her closely, as if trying to decide whether she was a friend or a foe.

Heather noticed and slowed her steps. "Is he okay with strangers?"

"Depends on the stranger. He's got good instincts," Brian answered.

Flash paused at her side, gave her a quick once-over, then trotted ahead and plopped down by the bench as if giving his approval.

"Well," Heather said with a laugh, "I guess I passed the test."

"Seems like it," Brian said, smiling as they sat. He then offered a brief explanation. "I'm fascinated by beauty in its raw, natural state. Like... with no filters or color. Just form and contrast. If you're willing to really look, there's something powerful in the simplicity."

Heather listened, trying to process his words. Her thoughts bounced in a dozen directions. *Is he serious? Is this some elaborate joke?* A part of her wanted to laugh it off, but another part couldn't help but be curious.

She tilted her head and said, "So... you're saying people just need to open their minds and... what? Find beauty in what looks like nothing?"

Brian's eyes lit up. "That's just it. People see a leafless tree and think decay, loss, emptiness. But I see structure, you know? Survival... Stillness. I think there's beauty in the bare bones of things. You just have to stop expecting it to shout at you in color."

Heather smiled, clearly intrigued. "You really believe that?"

"I do," he said simply. "There's honesty in the things we usually overlook."

Heather leaned back, folding her arms. "Huh. I always thought black-and-white was just... old. Like something out of a history book."

Brian grinned. "Maybe I'm a little old-school. Or maybe I just like reminding people that beauty isn't always obvious."

Heather paused and watched him thoughtfully. "You know," she said, "you might be the first person I've met who talks about photography like it's poetry."

Brian laughed softly. "Maybe it is. You just need the right lens."

As they talked, the conversation flowed from life in New York to the weather and even politics. Both Brian and Heather could sense a growing attraction. It didn't really matter what they were talking about; they were enjoying each other's company.

Heather tucked a strand of hair behind her ear and leaned back slightly on the bench. "I actually went to Boston College," she said. "Mostly because I'm from Boston originally, so it made sense to stay close to home."

Brian nodded. "Ah, that explains the accent I couldn't quite place."

She chuckled softly. "Guilty. After graduation, I wanted to work in social services—families, kids, that kind of thing. I interviewed with a few nonprofits, worked for two… but something just felt off."

"Off how?" Brian asked.

"I don't know." She glanced down at her hands. "Like maybe I wasn't doing *enough*. I started thinking about grad school, maybe becoming a licensed therapist instead. But the idea of staying in Boston forever?" She shook her head. "Didn't feel right either."

"So, you left?"

"Yeah," she said. "Wanted a bigger city, but still somewhere on the East Coast. New York felt like the right kind of overwhelming."

Brian chuckled. "That's one way to describe it."

"Yep. So here I am," she sighed. "Still trying to figure things out, honestly. But I started taking these long walks through the park. It clears my head."

There was a short pause before she added, a little shyly, "Actually… I've seen you and Flash a couple of times before. I just never said anything."

Brian raised a brow. "Really?"

"Yeah," she said with a soft laugh. "I didn't know what you were doing, honestly. You were always so focused… I figured you were either an artist or a little strange."

"Or both," he teased.

"Apparently," she grinned.

They talked for a few more minutes, exchanging stories about school, career dreams, and the strange paths that brought them to the same bench on that autumn afternoon. Then Heather glanced at her watch and sighed.

"Oh no, I'm going to be late. I've got dinner plans," she said, standing.

Brian stood too and extended his hand. "I get it. It was really great talking with you."

As they shook hands, Heather paused, still holding his hand for a moment longer than necessary.

"I actually learned a lot from you just now," she said. Then, almost before she realized what she was doing, she reached into her coat pocket and pulled out her phone. "Here… if you want to stay in touch."

Brian blinked, a little surprised, but smiled. "I'd like that."

They exchanged contact information, and then Heather left the park.

Brian sat back down and invited Flash to join him on the bench. Flash jumped up immediately, settling beside his partner and looking up at him. No words were spoken between them. They simply sat together, quietly, on a park bench with no one around.

After about fifteen minutes, Brian finally said, "Time to head home."

Flash jumped down, and they left the park. As they walked, Brian played their conversation over again in his mind, wondering if he and Heather would ever see each other again.

Chapter 9: Humming All the Way Home

For the remainder of that autumn, Brian and Flash continued making their way through Central Park, with Brian always on the lookout for something unusual and beautiful to photograph. Each time, he had to mentally convert what he saw in color into black and white, imagining how the scene would translate on film before deciding to capture it.

But something was changing. Brian was growing bored with the way he was going about his work. It was becoming harder to believe that anyone else might actually see the beauty he saw in his images. Even worse, he was growing bored with staying exclusively in Central Park, even though it was the largest park near where he lived and offered an abundance of photo subjects.

And there was another problem. While he had been focusing on his photography, he'd tried to push thoughts of Heather into the far corners of his mind. But it wasn't working. She kept resurfacing in his thoughts. He began taking more breaks, and deep down, he knew something, maybe several things, would have to change.

One day, back in Central Park, at a time when he would normally be immersed in hunting for the perfect shot, he wandered over to a bench and sat down. Flash jumped up beside him, sensing something was different. After fifteen minutes or so, Brian tucked his camera into his backpack, glanced at Flash, and said, "That's it for today, pal." Flash hopped off the bench, ready to follow Brian's lead. To Flash's surprise, they headed back to the apartment, something they almost never did in the middle of a perfectly fine photo-taking day.

Once home, Brian pulled out a notebook and began jotting down his thoughts. He made a list of what he felt he had accomplished so far toward his goal of creating a photo collection worthy of a gallery. He added "living independently" to the list. Then he paused.

Suddenly, it struck him: maybe living independently wasn't all it was cracked up to be. Why? Because Heather was still in his thoughts. And now, he realized he wanted to spend more time with her.

For a few moments, Brian wondered if he'd eaten something that was making him lose focus. His energy felt off, and he even started to sweat. *What is happening?* He thought. He made sure Flash had food and water, then headed to the couch to take a nap. The fatigue came on so suddenly, he felt like he might pass out if he didn't lie down.

An hour later, Brian woke up abruptly. He checked the time, momentarily confused about where he was, and why. But it all came back to him. And that's when he knew what he needed to do next. Two new goals had just joined the list. He wrote them down without hesitation:

Travel outside the New York area, maybe out west.

Get to know Heather better.

Actually... a lot better. But maybe not in that order.

Brian had only met Heather face-to-face once during their first meeting in the park. Since then, they had been communicating through text messages and the occasional phone call. Now, more than two months had passed since that day. That had to change, and Brian knew it. He was also aware that Heather had shown remarkable patience with him, giving him space, as if she instinctively knew he needed it.

That evening, Brian reached out to Heather and asked if she would like to meet for a drink, somewhere she would feel comfortable, preferably not far from her apartment. After what felt like an eternity, her response came in a single word: **"Yes!"**

They agreed to meet at a popular café that had a bar and catered to people their age. The music was never too loud, and it was the kind of place where you could actually have a conversation, maybe over a drink or some food.

When Brian arrived and stepped inside, he spotted Heather sitting in a booth facing the door, clearly watching for him. She smiled and gave a small wave to catch his attention, and it worked. Brian nodded to the host, explaining he was meeting someone who was already there, and made his way to the booth.

"Hey," Heather greeted as he approached. "Right on time."

Brian smiled as he slid into the seat across from her. "Wouldn't miss it."

She picked up her menu but didn't look at it. "This place has great reviews."

Brian leaned back slightly, settling in. "Sounds perfect. I could use a night of good food and even better conversation."

The next few hours flew by. Brian and Heather took turns talking about their families, childhood memories, college highs and lows, the weather, sports, and the professional futures they each envisioned.

They had met at 8 P.M. and were both surprised when they glanced at the time and realized it was midnight. Neither of them had eaten or drunk much. The conversation had simply taken over, and that was seemingly what mattered most.

Then suddenly, they both stopped talking at the same time, realizing what had just happened, and burst out laughing, as if they could read each other's mind. It hadn't been about the drinks or the food. It was about being in each other's company. And they both knew it. They also realized they were tired. It had been a long day for both of them. There was a brief pause, warm but heavy with the quiet acknowledgment that the night was winding down.

Brian shifted slightly in his seat. "I probably should get going. I left

Flash alone longer than I usually do, and he's probably pacing the apartment thinking I've abandoned him."

Heather nodded. "Of course. Poor guy."

Brian stood slowly, hesitating for a second. "But seriously… tonight's been amazing. This has been the best evening I've had in a very, very long time."

Heather looked up at him. "Really?"

He smiled. "Really."

"I feel the same," Heather said softly. "Let's not wait another two months before we do this again, okay?"

"Deal," Brian said, standing as she slid out of the booth beside him.

Brian stood and waited for Heather before walking with her past the reception stand and out onto the sidewalk. They paused. It was that awkward moment every couple experiences when sparks are flying.

Brian leaned in, gently kissed Heather on the cheek, and said softly, "I'll be in touch again soon. Very soon. I promise."

Heather, still smiling, returned his hug and whispered, "I'll hold you to that."

She turned and walked toward her apartment just a few blocks away, while Brian stayed behind for a moment, watching her go. Then he headed home too—briskly, humming to himself.

Humming. What? He never did that.

He couldn't wait to tell Flash about his evening.

Chapter 10: The Girl from Boston

Heather Parker was born and raised in Boston by a family with an above-average income. They were financially comfortable and encouraged Heather to pursue whatever made her happy in life. She had always been told they would support her financially, at least until she met someone who could, and would, provide her with the happiness she deserved. Perhaps they felt this way because Heather was their only child.

Her parents, Robert and Doris, were also originally from Boston. Robert was now a retired dentist. Doris spent her adult life after college working as an account manager in various office positions, mostly in the health care industry. They both retired three years ago and had since been traveling, mostly around Europe and on cruises.

Golf had always been Robert's passion, and it remained his full-time focus in retirement. He played as often as the weather allowed. Doris formed friendships with the wives of Robert's dental partners and a few neighbors. She also became involved in local charities and nonprofit organizations, regularly giving her time to help others.

As an only child, Heather never had to deal with sibling rivalry, but she also missed the closeness of having someone her own age at home, other than the children she saw at school. Despite having lived in Boston her entire life, she never felt particularly connected to the city's history or anything it had to offer. As a result, Heather grew up feeling somewhat lonely.

She began dating boys in high school, but those relationships were mostly friendships. In college, she believed, on two occasions, that she had met someone who might someday be "husband material," but neither relationship lasted long, and it was usually Heather who ended them. She had a natural curiosity about so many things that no one else seemed to care about, which made it hard for her to form a serious personal connection with most of the people she met.

She chose sociology and psychology as her main areas of study in college, believing that one day she might feel called to help others. Heather was well aware she came from an above-average-income family that lived a life of privilege by many standards. At various points in her young adult life, she felt a responsibility to give back to the community and to those less fortunate.

Her decision to leave Boston and move to New York wasn't difficult. She had never formed deep roots or strong personal connections to anything, or anyone, aside from her parents and a few distant relatives, all of whom lived in or near Boston. She was bored and felt the need to grow in an unfamiliar place, one with a different energy and a more active lifestyle, something that would push her beyond her comfort zone.

It was during this period of readjustment and exploration in New York that she first met Brian.

Her immediate fascination with him, his love of photography and his quest to do something outside the box by capturing unusual images in interesting settings—caught her attention right away. Heather felt a natural connection to Brian, one she neither understood nor tried to analyze. It just felt right. And with him, she felt safe.

As time passed, Heather remained mindful that she had never been truly happy living in Boston, but now, she felt something different, especially since meeting Brian. She tried to keep her thoughts and emotions in check, yet couldn't help but wonder where this might be heading. She reminded herself to stay present, but still giggled at the thought of someday settling down with someone like Brian, someone who, in such a short time, had captured her imagination and left her wanting more.

Chapter 11: The Business of Falling in Love

During the weeks Brian and Heather began dating, they kept things casual and moved slowly toward building a relationship rooted in trust, leaving romance out of the equation, at least initially. Neither had spoken directly about their feelings, but that didn't seem necessary. They were simply enjoying the rare experience of talking with someone who had a genuine interest in who they were as individuals, without pressure or expectations to rush the relationship forward. Perhaps that's why, and how, they had already been seeing each other longer than they had with anyone else in their respective pasts.

One evening, while having dinner at a casual restaurant not far from Heather's apartment, Brian opened up about his growing frustration.

Brian pushed his plate aside and let out a quiet sigh. "You know, I've been feeling... stuck lately."

Heather looked up from her meal. "Stuck how?"

"With my photography," he said, running a hand through his hair. "I've got this growing collection... like hundreds of shots I'm proud of. But I still don't feel ready to show them. Or sell them. It's frustrating."

Heather nodded thoughtfully. "Don't you think you're being too hard on yourself?"

"Maybe," he admitted. "Or maybe I'm just scared. Putting them out there feels... personal. Vulnerable."

She smiled gently. "Everything meaningful is."

He smiled back. After briefly dwelling on it, he changed the subject and told Heather that, someday in the not-too-distant future, he'd like to do things they hadn't yet discussed, like meeting her parents. But he wasn't finished sharing. Brian went on to say he wanted to travel more, especially outside of New York.

Heather listened carefully. She heard his desires and understood them. To her, these weren't just casual comments, they were Brian's way of telling her, without explicitly saying so, that he wanted to take their relationship to the next level. She wasn't surprised. And she wasn't afraid to move forward, either.

They began discussing the order in which they should approach Brian's goals, and how to blend Heather into those plans so she could become a bigger part of his life.

Heather admitted she was unhappy with the jobs she had held in New York and was currently unemployed. Fortunately, she had access to funds from a trust left to her by a late grandparent, and even more financial support was available from her parents if needed. This gave her a rare freedom to go anywhere and do just about anything she wanted.

Now that she wasn't working, she had more time to spend with Brian. She had met someone she felt truly comfortable with, and from Heather's perspective, it was her opportunity to support Brian in achieving his goals as a partner. She believed that helping him find happiness would, in turn, bring her happiness too.

Intellectually, she understood what this meant: they were taking the next step in their relationship. Emotionally, she was ready to let nature take its course.

Heather and Brian agreed to meet at her apartment one evening soon to have a more serious discussion about each of their current short-term goals, and maybe create a plan for Brian, in particular, to start tackling the next items on his "to-do list." With Flash now part of the equation, and after seeing Heather's apartment for the first time, even Brian had become a bit happier.

The following week, over wine and cheese at Heather's apartment, they held a meeting that felt natural, perhaps a bit serious, but it led to a conversation about where they were headed as a couple. That, in turn, resulted in a sleepover for Brian.

"So," Heather said, sipping her wine, "what's first on your list, Mr. Aspiring Gallery Artist?"

Brian grinned. "Well, that depends. Do I go west to take those desert shots I've been dreaming about? Or do I meet your parents and risk complete emotional collapse?"

Heather laughed. "Wow, that's a toss-up. Emotional collapse might be safer than Utah."

They shared a look that said more than either of them could explain in words.

The next day, Brian and Heather spoke about moving forward together as a couple. They also went through the list of goals they had agreed to pursue.

Back at his apartment, Brian began culling through the hundreds of photos he had taken, all safely stored in his darkroom. His immediate goal was to select a group of images to take to several galleries in New York and see if he could negotiate an agreement with at least one to sell them on a consignment basis.

He narrowed his selection to two dozen photos and placed them in a box. Later that evening, he arrived at Heather's apartment with the box under one arm.

"I brought the goods," he said. "I've narrowed it down to about two dozen shots I think might be worth selling. I'd love your opinion, especially on which ones to actually go with, and how to price them."

Heather raised an eyebrow. "You're really doing this? That's amazing!" She opened the box and began flipping through the photos. "But just so you know, I have no idea how to price artwork."

"That's okay. Just give me your gut reaction. Like... maybe rate them? One to five? One being 'meh,' five being 'I'd hang this in my living room.'"

Heather grinned. "Alright, deal. I'll do my very best art critic impression."

Heather examined each photo carefully, then started rating them one by one on a scale from one to five.

"Okay, this one's a five. It's intriguing to say the least."

"That's from Coney Island at dawn," Brian said, nodding. "Good eye."

Heather smiled. "And this one? Two. Sorry, but I don't feel anything from it."

"That's fair," he said, scribbling notes. "I didn't feel much either, to be honest."

While selecting which photos to take to a gallery, Brian was also wondering whether he should prioritize going with Heather to Boston to meet her family or taking that trip out west with her first. He had been researching Utah as a destination, and since it was now early March, there was still some late-season snow as well as places of interest that didn't depend on weather—so snow wouldn't be a factor.

He realized he had never asked Heather if she knew how to ski, so he added that to his list of items to follow up on.

Brian and Heather began separate planning in preparation for their next meeting, which they scheduled for no later than the following week. Their relationship now had the feeling of a mutually beneficial business arrangement—an odd dynamic, but one that made sense for them.

At their next meeting, Brian, Heather, and Flash gathered at Heather's apartment. Takeout food served as dinner, and the focus was discussing Brian's plan.

As the meeting progressed, music from Heather's entertainment center played softly in the background, the lights were dimmed, and before they had even finished the items on their agenda, it had gotten late. Brian felt too tired to drive back to his apartment, so, with a little encouragement from Heather, he spent the night.

Flash may not have immediately understood what was happening, but Brian and Heather did. They had become a couple.

And the fact that Heather had mentioned that night that she didn't know how to ski? It didn't matter to Brian. She couldn't have cared less—and had to laugh about it herself.

Chapter 12: Signed, Sealed, Ski Trip

The next day, after Brian and Flash returned to their apartment, Brian had an agenda. Step one was to review his collection of photos, now narrowed to twelve thanks to Heather's suggestions. Next, Brian needed to determine which to try to sell first and create a price list for the photos, incorporating Heather's recommendations. He then increased each photo's price by fifteen percent. Brian felt she wasn't fully aware of the potential value of his work and wanted to see what he could get for them.

He also wasn't sure whether to approach the popular galleries where other photographers were selling their work, or to visit a gallery on the Upper West Side, where his only competition would be traditional art galleries that didn't feature much photography. He chose the second option, the gallery on the Upper West Side. Brian wasted no time calling the gallery and made an appointment for that same day to show his photos to the gallery manager, who was a calm and quiet-sounding man named Douglas.

With his mind made up, Brian shifted into preparation mode. He made sure Flash had plenty of water and some food, then loaded his photo portfolio into his Jeep. The gallery was about an hour away due to New York traffic, so Brian headed straight to his meeting. When he arrived, he found Douglas waiting for him. Brian laid out his portfolio and waited. His heart was pounding with a mix of anticipation and hope.

After about fifteen minutes of reviewing Brian's portfolio, Douglas smiled, shook his hand, and asked him to follow him to his office at the back of the gallery to sign some paperwork. Brian could hardly believe it. He had a gallery!

Brian didn't wait. Before he even reached his Jeep, he pulled out his phone and called Heather.

"Heather! You're not gonna believe this! I got in! The gallery wants to show my work."

"Are you serious?" she said, her voice lighting up.

"Dead serious. The manager said he'll call me if anything sells. But it's happening. It's real."

There was a beat of silence before Brian grinned and added, "So... you ready for the trip to Utah?"

"Yes!" she shouted without hesitation.

So, this became Brian's next project as soon as he got back to his apartment. He quickly began figuring out where to go, stay, ski, etc. He was getting really excited, not only because he felt confident Douglas would be calling soon with news of a sale, but also because he was looking forward to getting away from New York and spending time with Heather on vacation. Of course, Flash would be going too, which made planning a bit more complicated in terms of flying and accommodations, but Brian had no intention of leaving Flash behind.

Many skiers say March is the best month for skiing in Utah, and Park City's ski season typically runs from late November to mid-April. That part was easy to figure out. Locating a ski resort that would accommodate Flash was the third part of the puzzle. After spending a few hours on the internet and texting back and forth with Heather, Brian had a plan for their Utah getaway. He remembered the line from some movie: "I love it when a plan comes together." To say he was really, really excited was an understatement.

Brian began working on an itinerary for their travel and time away. After making calls to resorts and checking airfares, he concluded that the best approach was to make Day One, a Tuesday, their travel day to Park City, and maybe get some skiing in if they could. Day Two, a Wednesday, would be a full day of taking in all the resort had to offer and skiing as much as possible, weather permitting. Day Three, a Thursday, would be another day like Wednesday, skiing as much as possible, again weather permitting. Brian assumed they might have some poor weather on at least one of their days at the resort and didn't want their time in Utah to be too short. So, while they could make this a Tuesday-through-Thursday adventure, he planned their return for Friday. On Day Four, a Friday, they would pack up and return to New York. That would leave Saturday and Sunday to catch up on anything that needed attention, relax sore muscles, and get ready for the week ahead.

Brian also put together a list of what he and Heather already owned that they could pack, and what they would need to rent or buy once they reached the resort.

The resort where they'd be staying had a shuttle to and from Salt Lake City Airport, about a forty-minute ride, so they wouldn't need a car during their stay. That meant taking a rental car off his list of things to do. Brian then sent all of this information to Heather in an email.

One of the things they both needed to do was let their respective families know what they were doing, where they would be, etc. Heather called her parents. Brian called Amy. Fortunately, there were no issues raised by anyone, which Brian, secretly and mildly had been concerned about. He thought, *How would Amy feel? What would Heather's parents say? They haven't even met me yet.*

Somehow, this hurdle was cleared, and Brian proceeded to make the arrangements with the airline and resort. All of this meant the items he had on his to-do list had been accomplished!

Both Brian and Heather were excited about their upcoming trip and were counting the days until they were scheduled to leave. Both had some last-minute shopping to do, and then it was just a matter of waiting for the day to head to Park City.

During this time, Brian did some reflecting on the past year and how far he had come. His life was changing, and he felt confident it was for the better. He also knew that many of his friends from college had taken jobs they hated and would likely be jealous if they knew how his life was going. He was living on his own, had met Heather, and now he was on his way to a magical ski vacation with Flash and Heather so they could all start a new chapter in their lives.

Brian felt content, perhaps for the first time since the day he lost his parents. And deep down, he felt like things were only going to get better.

Chapter 13: In the Shadow of Mountains

The trip to Park City was uneventful and without issues. The flight was on time, their shuttle ride was as advertised, and the resort was even better in person than in the online ads. When Brian, Heather, and Flash arrived at the resort, they checked in and went to their assigned room to unpack. The room was larger than they expected, and the view of the mountains was unbelievable; it felt like an unexpected bonus!

However, they did need to make a few adjustments. They had to get used to the time change and the altitude. Brian had suggested a stay of four days and three nights, feeling they would have enough time to do everything they wanted and be ready to return home on day four. That now seemed like a good plan. As tired as they were just from getting to their destination, that did not dampen their enthusiasm to get on the slopes right away.

The resort had both a childcare facility and a pet care center, which was one of the reasons Brian had chosen it. Flash was dropped off while Brian and Heather hit the bunny slopes to see how bad they might be at skiing. Brian had only skied once with some friends back in college, and Heather had never skied in her life. They both agreed this was a smart way to start, especially when looking at the size of the hills in front of them.

Both Brian and Heather tired quickly, not having used the muscles needed for skiing in quite some time.

Brian groaned as he plopped down onto a bench near the bottom of the slope. "Okay, I officially forgot how much skiing hurts."

Heather laughed, out of breath as she collapsed beside him. "Oh my! My legs feel like Jell-O."

"I think the altitude's messing with me. And the time change maybe is making it even more difficult," Brian replied.

Heather pulled off her gloves. "So... we done?"

"Done," he grinned. "But hey, not bad for day one, right?"

"We fell and survived. Feels like high school all over again," Heather said, looking right into his eyes.

"Except better," Brian replied, looking back. "I've never felt like this before."

They were only on the slopes for about an hour before deciding to call it a day. But what a first day it had already been. They had spent time skiing downhill, falling, laughing, and acting like teenagers. Brian hadn't felt this way ever.

Back at the resort, after picking up Flash and returning to their room, Brian decided to call Amy to let her know they had arrived safely and were having a great time. Heather took her cue from Brian and did the same with her parents.

After changing into more comfortable clothing, Brian flopped onto the couch and asked, "Alright. What are our dinner plans?"

Heather pulled up the resort menu from the side table. "There are a few restaurants here, but I don't think Flash is going to blend in with the wine-and-cheese crowd."

"Yeah," Brian laughed. "I don't want to spend dinner worrying about whether he's chewing on someone's napkin."

"Room service it is, then," Heather decided and picked up the phone to order dinner.

The three of them ate and enjoyed some quiet time, looking out the windows of their room at the lights on the mountain. All three were tired, and it didn't take long for slumber to snatch them away from their sense of tranquility.

***

Brian awoke before Heather the next morning and found Flash sitting nearby, looking at him and wagging his tail. He needed to go out, and he was hungry. Heather was still asleep when Brian and Flash took a brief walk, but by the time they returned, Heather was in the shower. A new day was waiting for all of them to explore and simply let things unfold.

They ordered breakfast from room service, having packed food for

Flash, and once no one was hungry anymore, they began preparing for their first big, full day doing what they came to do: ski. This time, they asked for permission to bring Flash along and received it. He was a perfectly behaved dog, and even the hotel staff remarked that they had never heard him bark. The staff also noticed Flash was always "under control," so they couldn't say no.

Since the day Brian and Flash were paired, Flash had barely ever barked, and when he did, it was only to alert Brian. As border collies go, he was on the small side and a low-maintenance pet. Brian and Flash had bonded so deeply that Flash had become almost an extension of Brian's emotions. Flash was also bonding with Heather, somehow understanding that she was now "part of the family."

Day Two brought a new experience: skiing with a dog. Until now, Brian and Heather had assumed they'd stick to the lower slopes, thinking putting Flash on a ski lift wouldn't be possible, or even safe. But this lodge had two types of ski lifts, including one with a bench seat that could accommodate Flash.

So, off the three of them went to one of the more challenging slopes. At first, Flash was a bit jittery, but soon his mood changed, and he found this new way of traveling uphill pretty interesting. If dogs could think in a way humans could understand, Brian and Heather might've known that Flash was wondering what all the other dogs he'd met in Central Park during his walks with Brian would say if they could see him now!

They reached the top of the slope and managed to get off the bench safely, ready for the next challenge. Brian and Heather had skis; Flash would need to run through the snow to keep up. But they had to try it—so off they went, all three of them.

The morning came and went, and soon it was time for lunch. It was a bit warm for a day of skiing, but Park City can get warm enough to enjoy the sunshine without the snow melting. They found an outdoor café where Flash could join them, and the three of them had lunch together.

Heather leaned back in her chair and lifted her face toward the light. "You know," she said in a calm voice. "I don't think I've felt this relaxed in... years."

Brian set down his fork and looked at her. "Yeah. Same. I wasn't sure coming here was the right move at first. I mean, skiing, mountains, leaving everything behind for a bit… for a moment, even a thought of maybe I'm running from things crossed my mind."

Heather turned her gaze toward him. "Sometimes it's okay to run, as long as you're running toward something that matters."

Brian smiled faintly. "Like sunshine, snow, and sandwiches with you?"

She laughed. "Exactly. And Flash," she added, reaching down to scratch behind the dog's ear. "Can't forget the fourth wheel in this three-wheel ride."

Brian looked down at Flash and chuckled. "He's probably the most grounded of the three of us."

A quiet passed between them. It wasn't awkward at all.

"You think," Heather began slowly, "that this trip... this time together... might be one of those moments we don't realize is important until later?"

Brian looked out toward the mountains, then back at her. "I think," he said, "we'll look back on this one day and wish we could freeze it right here."

Heather reached across the table and gently touched his hand. "I'm glad we came. I don't think I've seen you this at ease in... maybe ever."

"This was a great idea," Brian said at last. "Coming here. Not knowing exactly how things would turn out... might've been the best part."

Heather turned to him, smiling softly. "It turned out better than I imagined."

If someone had passed by just then with a camera and had captured the stillness, the tacit peace between the two of them, the mountain light catching in Heather's hair, the ease on Brian's face and Flash peacefully curled up at their feet, it would have been one special photograph.

After lunch, the weather suddenly changed. Clouds rolled in, the wind picked up with some fairly significant gusts, and then it began snowing. A member of the ski patrol, James Beal, happened to pass by where Brian, Heather, and Flash had just finished eating and stopped to chat.

"Hey there," James called out with a wave. "Mind if I say hello?"

"Not at all," Brian replied.

The man knelt beside Flash and petted him. "Now this guy's not something you see every day on the mountain."

Heather laughed. "He's probably the only one here without skis."

"He's beautiful," the man said, giving Flash a good scratch behind the ears. "Name's James, James Beal. I'm with the ski patrol."

"I'm Brian," he replied, extending a hand. "This is Heather. And Flash, of course."

"Pleasure. You two aware of the front that's rolling in?"

They both shook their heads.

James nodded toward the thickening clouds. "It's moving in quicker than expected. We're looking at stronger winds, reduced visibility… could get dicey up on the slopes. Couple folks already came down early. By the hour mark, it's gonna be a mess up there."

Brian looked out toward the lifts, already seeing fewer people heading uphill. "That fast, huh?"

"Afraid so," James said. "Might be safer to call it a short day on the mountain. How long do you guys plan to stay?"

Heather glanced at Brian, then back at James. "We just got here yesterday. Planning to stay a few more days, though."

"Well, that's perfect then," James said with a grin. "Plenty of time to get your runs in. Some folks are already calling it a wash for the afternoon. There's a makeshift casino being set up inside the resort."

"A resort casino?" Brian raised an eyebrow. "Woah."

James chuckled. "It's more poker chips than Vegas lights."

"Thanks for the heads-up," Heather said.

"Stay warm," James said as he stood and brushed snow from his jacket. "And keep an eye on the sky. The weather's turning fast."

With a nod and a pat on Flash's head, James continued down the path to speak with another group.

Brian turned to Heather. "Well, that answers the question of skiing this afternoon."

She nodded. "Yeah, that's definitely off the table now."

Brian smiled. "Exactly the kind of thing I had in mind when I planned for a few extra days here. Flex time."

Heather paused, watching the snow fall. "I'll be honest, I've never really been into casino games. Or any games, really."

"No?" Brian teased. "Not even charades?"

She smirked. "Especially not charades."

"Fair enough," Brian responded, laughing.

Heather pulled her scarf tighter. "You think we could rent a car? Drive around a bit? Maybe even check out Salt Lake City including the Church of the Latter Day Saints compound? Y'know... do the touristy thing?"

Brian tilted his head. "That's not a bad idea."

"It beats pretending to be excited about losing fake money to strangers," she said.

"Adventure over blackjack. I like it," Brian replied.

Flash let out a small huff, as if approving the plan himself.

Brian suggested that Heather and Flash head back to their room while he spoke with the resort staff about renting a vehicle for the day. It was something he hadn't thought to check when he first made their reservations.

As it turned out, the resort had a rental service on-site and was more than happy to help them arrange for a four-wheel-drive SUV. Brian thanked them for the information but held off on finalizing anything. He wanted to confirm with Heather first, just to be sure that a spontaneous road trip was how she wanted to spend the rest of their second day in Utah.

After returning to the room and discussing things with Heather, Brian called the vehicle rental center and made a reservation for a four-wheel-drive vehicle for the rest of the day. Once the arrangements were confirmed, Brian and Heather packed their backpacks for the trip. With Flash by their side, they went to pick up the car.

As it turned out, their idea wasn't exactly original. They managed to get the last available vehicle and were thankful James had given them a heads-up about the changing weather. They decided to skip Park City and drive to Salt Lake City to go on an adventure instead.

Along the way, the snow and wind picked up, reducing visibility. They realized they had made the right decision. Once they dropped in altitude and arrived in Salt Lake City, the weather cleared. It was less windy, so they decided to visit the famous LDS compound, as it was called.

As they approached, they were stunned by the size of the area and the architecture of the buildings in particular. They parked and entered the compound with Flash, receiving a few strange looks. Brian hadn't thought to ask for permission beforehand if he could bring Flash. He approached an elder and asked if Flash could remain with them rather than wait in the car while they visited. The elder hesitated, then smiled and granted permission with one exception. Flash would be allowed everywhere except inside the main building, which was off-limits to animals.

Brian, Heather, and Flash wandered around the compound while Brian took photos of the buildings. He had a desire to spend even more time taking photos of the Assembly Hall. The design was striking, and the stained-glass windows were especially unique. He was particularly curious about one feature: on each of the four sides of the gabled roof, one window displayed a circle with a six-pointed star inside. Each star was identical and resembled the Star of David.

Intrigued, Brian approached a guide to ask about the windows. All the guides inside the compound were teenagers wearing white shirts and black ties, both the boys and the girls. Brian asked one of the boy guides if there was any special significance to the unusual window feature. The boy looked up, then said he had no idea. He explained that Brian would need to ask an elder, as no one had ever asked him that question before.

The boy, whose name was Michael, walked across the grounds to speak with an elder. Brian watched as Michael relayed his question. The elder, dressed in a white shirt, black tie, and black suit, glanced at Brian, then walked over to join two other elders nearby. The three of them spoke quietly while occasionally looking up at the gable roof and the windows of the Assembly Hall. Brian found it puzzling that they seemed to be discussing the matter for so long. Shouldn't they have known the answer immediately?

After about fifteen minutes, Michael returned and told Brian that no one had ever asked that question before, and none of the elders could offer an explanation. Then he handed Brian a few pamphlets about the church and walked away.

Brian glanced back at the three elders, who were still silently watching him. Had he asked a sensitive question? He shrugged off the thought, exhaled through his nose and folded the pamphlets in half, slipping them into his coat pocket. Before he could say more, Heather stepped forward and turned to another guide who had just walked past.

"Excuse me," she said with a smile, "is there any chance we could see the organ that's played during the Sunday broadcasts? The one the Mormon Tabernacle Choir uses?"

The guide stopped and shook his head with practiced regret. "Oh, no, I'm sorry. That part of the compound is only open to visitors on Sunday mornings at eight sharp."

Heather raised an eyebrow. "Eight a.m., huh?"

"Yep. And even then, no pets allowed. Service animals, maybe, but not regular dogs."

Heather glanced down at Flash, who was sitting politely at her side. "Well," she murmured, "looks like we're not hearing a note of music today."

When Heather relayed the information about the organ tour to Brian, he gave a small nod.

"Well," he said, glancing around the square, "seems like we've seen about all we can here."

"Yeah," Heather agreed. "I think so."

Brian smiled. "How about lunch downtown, then maybe a drive through the city? We've got the car for the day… might as well explore a bit before we head back."

Heather looked up at the sky. The clouds had begun to regroup, drifting in slowly from the mountains. "Good idea. And we probably shouldn't stay too long down here anyway. It was snowing in Park City when we left, remember?"

Brian followed her gaze. "Right. The sooner we start heading back up, the better. I don't want to get caught in anything."

Heather gave Flash a quick scratch behind the ears. "Alright, buddy. Time for a little urban adventure."

Flash gave a soft bark in response. And with that, they all headed for the gate to exit the compound. Brian glanced back once more toward where the elders had been standing. They were still there, all three of them, not speaking, and not looking away when they saw Brian look back. He felt a twinge of discomfort, wondering why his simple question had stirred so much interest.

Brian, Heather, and Flash, or "The Three Amigos," as they had begun to call themselves, headed downtown in search of a lunch spot. They had no trouble finding food, but weren't welcomed inside any restaurant with Flash. So, they searched for a fast-food place, found one, and used the drive-thru to get their meals. Then they looked for a place to picnic. Brian spotted a park with benches and decided it would have to do. He parked the SUV, and the Three Amigos walked to a bench for their picnic, something Flash was certainly used to doing with Brian and Heather.

After lunch, Brian took advantage of the new surroundings and snapped a few photos in the park before they got back into the SUV to drive around a bit, then returned to Park City.

As they merged onto the highway, Heather broke the silence. "To be honest, I didn't feel entirely comfortable back at the compound."

Brian raised an eyebrow. "Really? What part?"

"It was just… a feeling," she said, shifting slightly in her seat. "I felt out of place. People were staring, and I don't know… it felt off."

Brian nodded slowly. "You're probably right. Bringing Flash might've been part of it. And maybe that question I asked threw one or more of the elders off balance."

Heather turned to him. "Yeah, maybe. But it wasn't just that. There was this… stiffness, like we were being watched the whole time."

He glanced at her, then back at the road. "Try not to let it get to you. Let's not allow that one experience to ruin our day."

Heather exhaled, then nodded. "You're right."

"Exactly," Brian said, offering a small smile. He reached for her hand, brushing it softly before giving it a gentle, reassuring press.

Nothing more was said about their visit to the compound. The drive back into the mountains toward Park City was a bit tricky. The higher they climbed, the heavier the snow fell, making visibility difficult. It took them twice as long to get back in the SUV as it had in the shuttle earlier that week, but they arrived safely. Brian was exhausted from the drive, and Heather could see it. She suggested they check the SUV back in and call it an early day.

She added that they should retreat to the warmth and comfort of their room and order room service for dinner. The room had a fireplace they hadn't yet used, and Heather suggested they finally light it. They both wondered how Flash would react to a fire in a small space.

Once back in their room, Brian and Heather changed into loungewear for the evening and lit the fireplace as planned. Flash sat up at first, staring at the flames, then looking back at Brian and Heather, then back at the fire. Eventually, he settled onto the little bed they had packed for him and fell asleep.

Despite not skiing much that day, they were all tired and asleep earlier than they ever would have been back in New York. It seemed everyone was worn out, no doubt from the altitude and the events of the day.

Chapter 14: Tracks in The Snow

Day three found Brian, Heather, and Flash up early, ready to give adventure skiing another try. The weather had taken a major turn for the better. The snow had stopped, the wind had calmed, and blue skies stretched overhead. Fresh white snow blanketed the landscape, calling them out to play.

As soon as breakfast was out of the way, the Three Amigos headed for the slopes, eager to pick up where they had left off before the weather changed their plans the day before. Dressed for the slopes and carrying backpacks stocked with fluids and snacks, they were well prepared. Brian also had his camera in tow.

They took the bench lift again, and when they reached the top, the scenery was even more breathtaking than on their first day. Off they went, more steady, confident, and noticeably faster. Flash had no trouble keeping up, bounding joyfully through the snow as Brian and Heather glided down a trail they hadn't explored before. This one had fewer trees and fewer people, giving them the freedom to experiment with their turns and speed. For snow skiers, this had to be considered a perfect day.

After about two hours on this particular run, followed by some cross-country-style skiing at the bottom, Brian and Heather decided it was time to stop for lunch. They both noticed that while Flash was clearly having the time of his life, he needed a bit of hydration and rest. So, they made their way across the area to a bench lift heading back up the slope. They hopped on and called it a morning.

At the top, they removed their skis and headed to the outdoor café for lunch. Sitting together, Brian and Heather began to look at each other as if they were meant to be together. They didn't need to say much... words weren't necessary in that moment. They finished their lunch, made sure Flash was well-fed and hydrated, and wore what seemed like permanent smiles.

Couples who've built lasting marriages often reach a point where they can finish each other's sentences. They understand what the other person is thinking without having to ask. This was one of those moments.

After lunch, the trio took their time, lounging on a snow-dusted bench near the lodge as they let their meals settle.

Heather stretched and yawned. "I don't know about going back to the lift just yet. I feel like a stuffed turkey."

"Same," Brian said, chuckling. "Maybe we skip the downhill and do something a little lighter?"

"Cross-country?" she suggested. "We'd still get the exercise, and Flash wouldn't have to plow through deep snow."

Brian looked down at Flash, who wagged his tail as if he already approved. "Alright, buddy," Brian grinned. "Let's find a trail."

They started out away from the resort, heading toward a wooded area. After about thirty minutes on a pristine trail, they found themselves in a remote part of the resort grounds with no one else around. It was quiet and sunny, with a gentle breeze blowing. The snow remained untouched, which was evidence that no one had been on this trail that day.

"Listen to that," Heather said in a lowered voice with awe. "Nothing but the breeze."

Brian smiled. "This is perfect."

Then, without warning, Flash stopped. He stood still for a beat as his ears perked. Then he turned and padded deliberately toward a tree line, heading away from the trail.

"Flash?" Brian called. "Where are you going, bud?"

Flash didn't even glance back.

"That's weird," Heather murmured, slowing to a stop.

Flash paused near the edge of the trees, turned toward them, and barked once.

Brian and Heather exchanged glances.

"He doesn't usually bark like that," Heather said, frowning. "Do you think he found something?"

Flash looked down at the snow, then back up. Another bark. Then two more, quick and urgent.

"Okay, something's up," Brian muttered, already gliding off the trail toward Flash. "Let's go."

They moved carefully over the snow until they reached him. Flash had stopped and sat, staring at the ground.

Brian crouched beside him. "What is it, boy?"

Then he saw it, tracks in the snow. Human footprints. Out here?

"Someone's been through here," he said, puzzled. "But this trail looked untouched…"

Heather leaned in closer. "Brian… is that… blood?"

There, just ahead of Flash's paws, were several small, dark red drops speckled in the snow.

Brian's heart stopped for a beat. "Yeah. Looks like it."

Heather went quiet. She just stared at the snow where Brian knelt.

Brian stood slowly and scanned the trees beyond. "What did you find, Flash?"

Flash didn't move. He just kept staring into the woods.

Brian stood up, brushing snow off his gloves. "I think someone might be hurt."

Heather turned to him. "What do we do?"

"You go back," he said. "Head to the resort. Get ski patrol, or someone with first aid."

"What about you?" she asked quickly. "You're staying?"

Brian nodded, looking toward the trees again. "I don't want to walk any farther and mess up the tracks. And I sure don't want to leave if someone out there needs help."

Heather hesitated. "You sure?"

"I've got Flash. We'll stay put."

She gave one last glance at the red-stained snow, then back at him. "Okay. I'll be fast."

Brian watched her ski away. Then, he spoke quietly, mostly to himself. "What do you think, boy? Someone wandered off? Got hurt?"

Flash didn't bark this time. Just stayed still with his eyes locked on the tree line.

It took about thirty minutes for Heather and two members of the ski patrol to arrive and investigate what Brian, Flash, and Heather had seen. When the ski patrol reached the spot where Brian and Flash were waiting, they saw the footprints and the drops of blood.

One of the ski patrol members introduced himself as Hank and turned to Brian. "You're the one who found the prints?" Hank, asked.

Brian nodded. "Flash spotted them. We didn't follow them, just waited here."

The second ski patrol member crouched beside the snow. "Yep. Someone's definitely been through."

Hank stood. "Alright. You three stay right here. Keep the dog close."

Brian raised a brow. "You think it's serious?"

"We're about to find out," Hank said grimly. "Don't follow. We'll be back once we know more."

With that, the two ski patrol members began following the trail of prints and blood deeper into the trees. Brian watched them go until they vanished beyond the line of pines.

Heather folded her arms. "I don't like this."

Brian looked down at Flash, who hadn't budged. "Me neither."

Suddenly, Brian and Heather heard one of the ski patrol members speaking into his two-way radio, requesting an immediate response from the Park City Police Department and relaying their coordinates to the dispatcher on the other end.

Hank came toward them and said curtly, "I need to ask you both a few questions."

Brian gave a cautious nod. "Sure."

"Your full names, please?"

Heather exchanged a glance with Brian, then answered, "Heather Parker."

"Brian Miller," Brian added.

"Are you staying at the resort?"

"Yes," Heather replied. "Cabin 14, just off the north path."

"How long have you been guests?"

"This is our third day," Brian said.

"Phone numbers and email addresses?"

They both provided their contact information while Hank scribbled it all down. Then he looked up again, tone still clipped. "How did you end up in this part of the resort today?"

"We were cross-country skiing," Brian explained, gesturing at the smooth trail behind them. "Decided to skip the lift, figured it'd be easier for Flash in the flatter snow."

"He's our dog," Heather clarified.

Hank nodded slowly, but said nothing.

Brian frowned. "What's going on? Is someone hurt?"

"Can't say," Hank replied flatly. "Just stay here. The Park City police are on their way. You'll need to speak with them too."

Heather blinked. "Wait what? Why can't we leave?"

"Because the area's being treated as part of an active investigation," Hank said, turning slightly away and checking something on his phone. "Protocol. Please stay put."

Brian didn't answer. His eyes were fixed on the ridge Hank had returned from. Flash also sat quietly, staring in the direction of the footprints. Brian and Heather stayed where they were, waiting for someone to explain what was going on. About an hour later, two Park City police detectives arrived on skis and introduced themselves. They asked Brian and Heather to remain in place while they spoke with the ski patrol member who had stayed somewhere beyond the ridge, hidden behind the tree line.

Roughly ten minutes later, the detectives returned to find Brian and Heather still standing on their skis. They began asking the same questions Hank had asked over an hour earlier. At first, the detectives, like Hank, offered no explanation.

Another thirty minutes passed before more members of the Park City Police Department arrived, two of them carrying a stretcher, the kind used when someone has been in an accident and needs to be carried to safety. The detectives and one ski patrol member headed back across the snow into the tree line, while Hank stayed with Brian, Heather, and Flash.

When the detectives and ski patrol member returned, they were carrying what appeared to be a body in a zippered plastic bag. A forensic team had also arrived and had joined the detectives and ski patrol member beyond the tree line before everyone returned.

All were quiet, and no one was speaking. Then, one of the detectives stepped forward toward them. "Mr. Miller? Ms. Parker?" The detective removed his ski cap, revealing thinning gray hair. "I'm Detective William Hill," he said. "We'd like you both, and your dog, to come with us voluntarily for further questioning at the Park City Police Department."

Brian's eyes narrowed. "Why? You've kept us here for nearly two hours, asking the same questions. We're not going anywhere. Not until someone tells us what's going on."

The detective met his eyes without flinching. "We found a body," he said plainly. "A dead person. And we need to ask you both some questions. It might not seem like you know anything, but even something small, something you don't think matters, could help us."

Heather's legs gave out beneath her, and she sank into the snow with a soft gasp. Flash immediately padded over and pressed himself against her, licking her cheek, nuzzling into her lap.

Brian was dumbstruck and couldn't speak. He was suddenly flooded with the memory of getting the call from Amy to come to the hospital the day his parents were killed. He, too, went into mild shock.

The detective's voice broke through the fog, steady but gentler this time. "Look, I know this is a lot. But the sooner you come with us to the Park City Police Department, the sooner we can get through this, and the sooner you can go back to the resort."

Brian, Heather, Flash, and the two Park City detectives began the trek back to the resort. They stored their skis with the ski patrol and then rode to the police station in a patrol car as requested, saying nothing along the way.

Upon arrival at the station, Brian and Heather were told that the detectives needed to question them separately, in different rooms and at the same time, so they wouldn't have to remain there for long. Brian asked Detective Hill if they were considered suspects in connection with the death. Hill assured him this was standard procedure to gather information that might help them determine what had happened, and that they were not suspected of any wrongdoing at that time.

Brian and Flash were taken into one interview room, while Heather went into another with the second detective. The interviews lasted about an hour, with each detective questioning them independently.

Afterward, the two detectives met privately to compare Brian's and Heather's accounts of the day's events at the resort, including how they had spent their time in Utah.

As quickly as it had all begun, it was over. Brian, Heather, and Flash were provided transportation back to the resort. It was late afternoon, and there was no conversation during the ride.

When they reached the resort, Brian noticed a Salt Lake City news crew speaking with resort staff, clearly waiting to talk to him and Heather. As soon as they stepped out of the police car, Brian leaned over to Heather, took her hand, and whispered for her to stay close and not speak to the reporters, or anyone else. He just wanted to get Heather, Flash, and himself back to their room, where they could have the safe and quiet sanctuary they desperately needed. He felt completely drained and could see that Heather was just as shaken.

They were scheduled to fly back to New York the next day, but one of the detectives had mentioned they might need to return to the station for further questioning and advised them not to leave Park City. Brian objected but decided not to start an argument while technically still in the custody of Park City police, even though they were now back at the resort.

For the rest of what was left of the day, Brian, Heather, and Flash stayed in the quiet safety of their room. They instructed the resort staff that they were not to be disturbed by reporters or anyone else. They knew they needed time to recover from everything they had just experienced.

Did the police actually think they were responsible in some way for someone's death? They didn't even know if the victim was a man or a woman. Their nerves were raw, and they resented that their perfect vacation together had been so abruptly and rudely interrupted.

Brian then gently reminded Heather that someone had died on the resort property, and they needed to keep that in mind to be fair to the people who were only doing their jobs by questioning them.

Brian and Heather had a television in their room but chose not to turn it on or watch any news. They decided to order dinner from room service and spend the rest of the evening trying to relax. By the time dinner arrived, they had come to the conclusion that their little trip had been a complete success, until they discovered that a stranger had died. Still, they agreed not to let that ruin everything for them.

Brian had been given a business card by Detective Hill with his number on it, so he called, reached voicemail, and left a message saying that unless they were being charged with a crime, he, Heather, and Flash would return to New York the next day as planned. He also mentioned that his best friend was a big-shot attorney in New York and would be in touch if there was any issue. Brian conveniently left out the part Mike was actually a real estate, bankruptcy, and personal injury attorney, which completely cracked Heather up as she listened to Brian's message. It made them both laugh for the first time since they were pulled off the trail by Flash's barking, and it broke the tension.

Twenty minutes later, Brian's cell phone rang, and both he and Heather froze, fearing it might be the police. But the caller ID showed a New York number, not one from Utah, so Brian answered, wondering who it could be.

"Brian? It's Douglas from the gallery."

Brian blinked. "Douglas?"

"Yeah, sorry for the random call. I didn't think to text first."

"No, no, it's fine," he said, glancing at Heather with a confused shrug. "What's up?"

"Well, I wanted to give you some good news," Douglas said cheerfully. "Two of your photos sold today. Both from the tree series."

Brian sat up straighter. "Wait! Seriously?"

"Absolutely. Same buyer. Full price."

Brian let out a quiet, amazed laugh. "Wow. That's... that's amazing. Thank you for calling. I really needed that today."

"Glad I caught you," Douglas replied. "I'll email the paperwork over tonight."

"Perfect. I'm out of town at the moment, but I'll take care of it as soon as I'm back in the city."

They said a quick goodbye, and Brian ended the call.

Heather leaned in. "So?"

He turned to her with a smile spreading across his face. "Two photos sold today. Full asking."

Heather jumped up a little with joy and hugged him. "Brian, that's incredible."

"Right?" He laughed softly. "God, what timing. I didn't even have Douglas saved in my phone, or I would've picked up faster."

"Still. What a gift after the day we've had."

Brian reached for her hand. "You know, even with everything that happened, I've really enjoyed being here with you. All of it. Even the parts that made no sense."

Heather's gaze softened. "I was just thinking the same thing."

"Maybe we head back tomorrow as planned," he said. "No drama. Just go home."

Heather nodded. "Sounds right."

Brian paused as the word *home* echoed in his head. Then, carefully, he said, "Speaking of home… what does that word mean to you?"

Heather tilted her head. "Now or in general?"

"Now. Us." He hesitated. "I mean, I've been thinking. Maybe it's time I moved in."

She blinked, then smiled slowly. "Are you serious?"

"Well," he said, rubbing the back of his neck, "you've got space, light, an actual kitchen. A bathtub that doesn't make demon noises.

"Yeah. I do." She laughed. "And let's be honest, you're basically already living out of your camera bag at my place half the time."

"That's fair," he chuckled. "And we'd save money. Especially if I stop pretending I can justify rent in Manhattan."

Heather grinned. "Then yes. I'd love that."

Just then, Flash lifted his head from where he'd been resting by the fireplace. Slowly, he crawled over to them, wedging himself between their legs, pressing his head into Heather's thigh with a quiet sigh.

Brian looked down. "I think he's in favor."

Heather scratched behind Flash's ears. "He knows."

Despite the events of the day, the tension they'd been feeling melted away, and they were once again able to focus on their future.

Chapter 15: Boxes, Parents, and Big Questions

After Brian and Heather returned to New York, it took about a week for them to readjust. The time zone shift still left them a little off, even though they'd only been gone a few days. The altitude felt better too. That would have been normal after any trip if they hadn't gone through such a nightmare experience.

They were grateful they hadn't actually seen a body or been forced to try and save a life. On the morning of their flight, they had read in the *Salt Lake City Tribune* that an unmarried man had been found dead at a Park City ski resort under "suspicious circumstances." The article mentioned trauma to the upper body but gave no further details. The police never followed up with Brian or Heather, so the two decided to move on with their lives.

One evening, they sat in Heather's apartment, and the topic of moving in together circled back into conversation.

"It just makes sense," Heather said, curling her legs under her on the couch. "You're here most of the time anyway."

Brian nodded. "I've been thinking the same thing. I'll talk to my landlord. Maybe he'll let me out of the lease."

He did. Because Brian had been referred by someone the landlord trusted, and had been a model tenant, his landlord agreed to let him go without penalties. He liked Brian and understood the circumstances of his request.

By the next month, the decision was set. Brian had little furniture, and Heather's building had no issue with Flash. From both their perspectives, it was a relatively intelligent decision.

On a clear, dry day in April, Brian carried the last of his boxes up Heather's steps and officially changed his address. He notified Amy, Mike, and the post office. For both Heather and Brian, this was a major milestone in their relationship, and they did not take it lightly. Neither had ever lived with anyone except parents or casual roommates before. This called for a celebration.

That night, Brian took Heather out to dinner to celebrate.

"I just want you to know," he told her across the table, "this isn't casual for me. Not even close."

Heather smiled, though she looked a little nervous. "I know. It wasn't easy for me either. But…it feels right."

There was still the matter of telling her parents. Heather admitted she wasn't sure how they'd react. After all, she was their only child.

"And we still haven't gone to Boston," she added. "That has to be next. My folks need to meet you."

Brian nodded, though part of him bristled at the thought. "Yeah.

Sooner rather than later."

The waiter placed their desserts on the table, and they shared a quiet smile. For the first time in weeks, Brian felt like they were standing on solid ground, uncertain of what lie ahead, but certain about each other. Brian wondered how he had become so lucky.

The next morning after a trip to Boston had been discussed with Heather, Brian visited the gallery where his photos were still on display and learned that two more had been sold. He hadn't been notified and hadn't seen any funds deposited into his bank account. The gallery apologized and asked if he could provide more photos for sale. Of course, he agreed. That little piece of good news was added to his to-do list as a high priority. He also decided it was time to start asking a higher price for each new photo he submitted to the gallery.

By now, spring had arrived in New York, and the city was alive with its usual hustle and bustle, filled with visitors from around the world. That meant more traffic, especially in the parks. Once again, Brian had to reconsider whether to stay in Central Park for his photography or venture farther outside the city.

He chose the latter, exploring the small villages that dotted the Hudson River as it wound north into Westchester County, hoping to find new subjects to "target" besides benches and trees. Flash enjoyed riding shotgun, sticking his head out of the window to catch the fresh air rushing past. They made quite an interesting image together, slowly driving in and out of those small villages in their little black Jeep.

One idea kept nagging at Brian: finding an old, abandoned warehouse that he could photograph in summer, fall, and winter from the exact same spot, capturing the passage of time. As he mulled it over in his head, he suddenly saw it: a vacant, rundown red-brick building, three stories tall, its windows mostly boarded up, with just a few broken panes. It was perfect. He parked outside a padlocked chain-link fence and, with Flash at his side, carefully walked closer, watching his step to avoid anything sharp that might injure them. He also needed to figure out how to find the same exact vantage point once snow covered the ground in winter. After about an hour of exploring, he felt confident he'd found what he was looking for. It wasn't going to be an Andy Warhol soup-can moment, but framed correctly, it could become a breakthrough piece for his portfolio.

At the same time Brian was focused on his photography, Heather had to remind him about the trip they needed to take to Boston to meet her parents. He had, in a way, forgotten about it, though more accurately, he was avoiding the subject. Deep down, he feared that everything good between him and Heather could be put at risk if anything in Boston "went wrong." Despite his concerns, he agreed they should go and asked Heather to check with her parents about open dates in the near future. Heather only had to make one call to set it up. Her parents suggested that Brian and Heather stay in one of the extra bedrooms at their home.

When Heather relayed this to Brian, he was more than a little surprised. He hadn't even considered this scenario. To his surprise, they also invited Flash to join them on the trip. For Brian, planning the Utah trip had been exhausting, but Heather had made this one call and, just like that, he, Heather, and Flash were invited to the Parkers' in Boston, as though they were already married. *What did that mean?* Brian didn't mention anything about housing or transportation; he simply asked Heather to "handle it." And she did. On the one hand, he really wanted to meet her parents, but he also felt just a bit awkward about the arrangements. He stopped overthinking, asked Heather for the confirmed dates, and put them into his calendar. It was set for the following week.

The days leading up to the trip passed more quickly than Brian expected, and before long, the Brian, Heather and Flash were on the road. The drive to Boston went smoothly. Even Flash seemed to enjoy it, despite the four-hour ride. Meeting Robert and Doris Parker for the first time also went without incident. Heather's parents were warm and welcoming, treating Brian and Flash as if they had been part of the family for years. Brian and Robert spent time talking about Robert's career as a dentist, while Brian shared his goal of becoming a professional photographer. Meanwhile, Heather and Doris, who hadn't spent time together in a long time, decided to go shopping to mark the occasion.

Over the next couple of days, there were lunches, dinners, and plenty of conversation. Without ever saying it directly, Robert and Doris seemed to approve of Brian. It was obvious to Heather, and that in itself was no small thing. At one point, while Brian and Robert were in Robert's study having drinks and discussing business and life in general, Doris cornered Heather in the kitchen.

"Heather, is there anything else you want to share with me?"

Heather blinked, then gave a small laugh. "Mom, if you're asking what I think you're asking… no. Brian and I may be living together and we might be in a committed relationship, but we're still just dating. We haven't gone beyond that."

Doris tilted her head, clearly curious. "I see. You know, when your father and I were your age, we courted first, then got engaged. Living together didn't come until after marriage."

Heather nodded, trying to keep her tone gentle. "I know, Mom. Times are different now. But please, let's put that question in a drawer for another day. No offense, really."

For a beat, Doris studied her, then smiled. "Fair enough. Times have changed, and I'm cool with how you and Brian are doing things."

Relief washed over Heather, and she squeezed her mother's hand. "Thanks, Mom. That means a lot."

Little did Heather or Doris know, but Robert, though far more subtle, raised the same subject with Brian in the study. With a glass in hand and his tone casual, he leaned back in his chair and took full advantage of his adult and business skills.

"So, Brian," Robert said, "you and Heather seem pretty settled. Where do you see things going?"

Brian took a slow sip from his glass before answering. "Honestly, Robert, Heather and I are in a good place. We're committed to each other, but we haven't talked beyond where we are now. I respect her too much to rush that conversation before we're both ready."

Robert nodded, but his expression was unreadable. "Fair enough. I just want to know she's with someone who takes her seriously."

"I do," Brian said firmly. "More than anything. This relationship matters to both of us."

That seemed to satisfy Robert, and the two moved on to lighter conversation about business and photography. Brian didn't want to upset the apple cart, but he did want Robert to understand that his relationship with Heather was deeply important to them both, even if they hadn't discussed taking it beyond where it existed now.

Before long, it was time for Brian, Heather, and Flash to return to New York. Brian couldn't help thinking it might have been the shortest "get to know you" trip in history, but it had served its purpose. Heather was satisfied too. Mission accomplished, and Brian could finally take that item off his to-do list!

Chapter 16: Jackpot!

In the coming months, Brian, Heather, and Flash settled into new routines, unlike most young couples with a dog. Heather began joining Brian and Flash on their photo hunts, often bringing along a picnic basket so the three of them could take breaks together during the day. Brian also delivered more photographs to the gallery he worked with, selling at least one or two each week. The steady sales encouraged him to keep improving his craft.

As autumn approached, Brian made the decision to change how he took photos. With enough money saved, he bought a new, modern professional camera. It was a major departure from how he had started, but he also felt it was time to introduce color photographs into his portfolio. When he mentioned this to Heather, she had no strong opinion other than to say he should follow his instincts.

Brian shopped for and purchased a top-of-the-line mirrorless digital camera along with several excellent new lenses. He felt expanding his work was important to avoid being stereotyped as the photographer who only took black-and-white shots. Learning the new camera took practice, and he also had to convert part of the darkroom he used at Amy's apartment into a filing room for storing his digital photos. After about three weeks of practice, he finally felt comfortable enough to go after new subjects of interest and test whether his creative eye and brain could keep up with the change in how he now took photos.

On one particularly sunny, crisp autumn day, Brian, Heather, and Flash were in their favorite hunting ground—Central Park. The air was cool, and the leaves were in full Autumn glory. Brian kept glancing around for something worth photographing.

As they strolled along, Heather suddenly whispered, "Stop!"

Both Brian and Flash froze right where they were.

Brian whispered, "What is it?"

Heather pointed toward a bench under a canopy of oak, maple, and elm trees painted in red, yellow and gold. "Look," she whispered.

Brian followed her finger. A man sat there, head bent forward over a newspaper, pencil moving across what looked like a crossword puzzle. He hadn't noticed them at all.

"What a character," Brian murmured.

The man wore a worn, slightly torn bucket hat, tan corduroy pants that had clearly seen better days, a flannel shirt, and cowboy boots. It was a sight to behold.

Heather grinned. "He looks like he belongs here, like part of the scene."

Brian nodded slowly, taking in the kaleidoscope of colors framing the solitary figure. "A perfect setting."

Heather raised a brow and asked teasingly, "You're not really thinking about taking his picture, are you? He'll see."

"Not from here," Brian murmured, easing his camera strap off his shoulder. "I've got the right lens. I can frame the trees and bench, and keep his face hidden. If I ask, the moment's gone."

Heather sighed but kept quiet, understanding that look in his eyes. Since the man's head was down and his face was hidden, he couldn't be identified—something that eased any potential privacy issues if he later saw the photos Brian was about to take. If Brian ever sold the image and the man eventually discovered it, Brian would deal with that when the time came. For now, asking permission for a posed shot would ruin the moment. This was a perfect candid, unusually colorful scene.

Brian slowly raised the camera, adjusted the focus, and pressed the shutter. He adjusted the settings and took a few more, keeping in mind that he would not get a second chance to get this photo right. Finally, he lowered the camera with a grin tugging at his lips.

They backed away just as quietly as they had arrived, taking another path so as not to disturb the scene. Brian's heart was racing, fueled by the adrenaline of the moment and the breathtaking mix of bright colors made even more majestic by the clear azure sky. The sunlight provided the perfect light for the distance he had from his subject, and he had managed not to accidentally alert the man on the bench.

There had been plenty of times in the past when Brian thought he had captured the "perfect" photo, but this time felt different. Heather and Flash walked quietly on either side of him, sensing his excitement.

When he spotted a vacant bench, Brian, Heather and Flash each took a seat on it. Brian immediately lifted the camera to check his shots. He scrolled through the photos, and his grin widened.

"Well?" Heather asked.

"Heather… these are outstanding," Brian replied excitedly. "Andy Warhol, look out! Brian Miller just hit the jackpot!"

Heather chuckled, shaking her head. "You and your jackpot moments."

Brian held the camera out for her to see. "No, really. Look at that light, the balance, the colors. If this isn't perfect, I'll eat a hat of my own."

Heather peered at the screen, then smiled despite herself. "Okay, I'll admit it. That is something."

Brian leaned back against the bench, satisfied. For once, perfection had stood still long enough for him to catch it.

After some water and snacks, Brian, Heather, and Flash headed back to her apartment so he could process the day's work. His hands weren't steady enough to take more photos, and he knew it. There was something truly different about that last shot.

When they got home, Flash immediately flopped onto his bed, already drifting toward dreams. Heather stretched out on the only couch with a soft sigh of relief, while Brian slipped into his new home office to download the day's photos. As the images filled the larger screen, he leaned back, nodding in quiet satisfaction. The colors were even more vivid than he remembered, and one photo in particular seemed to glow with something rare and special. A smile spread across his face, but the longer he stared at the screen, the heavier his eyelids grew.

He thought about telling Heather he was going to lie down for a nap, but when he peeked in, she was already fast asleep. For a moment, Brian just stood there, taking in the calm around him. After the rush of the day, this quiet felt just as valuable. Fresh air, a beautiful day, a perfect photo, and his best friends… What a day!

Chapter 17: Man on a Bench

Brian decided to create a new and improved marketing strategy using his latest black-and-white photos, with his new color photo, *Man on a Bench,* as the centerpiece. He selected twelve of his best black-and-white photos, taken in different locations and featuring varied subjects that he had not taken to any gallery already, arranging them in a circle like numbers on a clock. In the center, he placed the single color photograph, *Man on a Bench*. It took Brian two days to get it "just right."

To complete the piece, Brian chose to have *Man on a Bench* matted and framed by a local framing shop he had worked with before. Proper matting and framing, he knew, could make all the difference when displaying art. When Brian and the framing shop completed *Man on a Bench*, it was designed so the black-and-white photos surrounding the color centerpiece could not be moved or rearranged. The matting was the key to making that possible. Once framed, it became a single piece of art—thirteen photos fixed in place as one.

Confident in his vision, Brian decided to approach a more upscale gallery that typically did not even sell photographs, only fine art. He wanted it to be somewhere in the small commercial district of New York's Upper West Side. Only one such place came to his mind, a gallery that called itself an "art studio." He planned to see if they would accept his new piece under the same or similar terms of arrangement he had negotiated with other Manhattan galleries.

This time, Brian priced the piece higher than anything he had sold before. In his mind, the value was justified both by the quality of the individual photographs and by the unique way they were displayed. If he was wrong, he could always separate them and try again with a different approach.

When everything was ready, Brian packed the photos into a portfolio case and drove to the art studio. He even dressed more carefully than usual—business casual rather than his typical relaxed style. Once he arrived, he parked his Jeep around the corner, out of sight of the studio. He thought perhaps pulling up in a little black Jeep might spoil the first impression he wanted to make with the studio owner.

After entering the studio, Brian slowly walked through, studying the various art pieces on display while patiently waiting for the owner to greet him. He was suddenly approached by a young woman with a slight Eastern European accent who introduced herself as Natalie, the studio owner's personal assistant.

Brian introduced himself and shook Natalie's hand. "I've got something I'd like to show the studio owner personally," he said, tapping his leather portfolio.

Natalie remained firm. "Part of my job is to screen everything that comes in. The owner's time is valuable, and I'm not allowed to let just anything through."

Brian paused and then smiled. "Fair enough. That's actually a smart strategy," Brian replied, realizing she was the gatekeeper he needed to win over. He then tilted his head slightly. "Is there somewhere I could lay this out for you?"

After a short pause, Natalie nodded and led him to a private room. Brian carefully pulled *Man on a Bench* from his case and placed it on the white laminated table. Then, without looking at Natalie, he stepped back slowly, folded his arms, and waited in silence.

Natalie leaned in, studying the work. "You personally took these? And created this entire piece?"

"Yes," Brian said simply.

She hovered over the photos for a long moment, then straightened. "Wait here."

She left the room, and Brian stood waiting. The next few minutes felt like hours. Finally, a tall, tanned gentleman with an ascot stepped in. He didn't look at Brian right away, but instead went directly to the table, gazing at the display for a long time before turning.

"You know we only show the best art in New York, don't you?" the man asked.

"Of course," Brian replied without hesitation. "That's exactly why I'm here." He extended his hand. "Brian Miller, and this is *Man on a Bench*."

118

"Rudy Glass," the owner of the studio said, shaking it firmly. "Sit, if you've got the time."

They sat across from each other, and Rudy began interviewing Brian. "Tell me about your background. Education. Your experience with art, photography, in particular."

Brian had been ready for this moment. He gave his pre-planned presentation, then added, "I could've brought other pieces before, but honestly, I didn't think they fit this studio's image or clientele. This collection does. I believe this gallery is the best place for it to be seen and purchased by someone who appreciates new and unusual art."

Rudy leaned back slightly. His tone softened, which gave Brian the hint that his presentation seemed to work. "Brian, would you care for some coffee? Or perhaps tea?"

Brian shook his head politely. "Thank you, Rudy, but I'll pass. My schedule's packed today." He smiled faintly, though he knew in truth—his day was wide open. "What I would suggest, though, is that we discuss how to structure and arrange a way to handle the sale of this collection, if you are indeed interested."

Rudy's lips curved into a smile. "Very well. Why don't you pack up *Man on a Bench* and follow me into my office?"

Brian carefully returned the piece to his leather case, then followed Rudy down a hallway into a richly decorated private office.

Rudy pulled out a folder, spread paperwork across his desk, and spoke as he wrote. "We'll put together a consignment contract. It'll include all the necessary information to make this binding." He finished filling it out, slid the pages across the desk, and tapped the signature line. "Read it over. If it works for you, sign."

Brian leaned in, scanned the contract with care, and nodded. It was exactly what he had hoped for. He picked up the pen and signed with confidence. Inside, he couldn't help but think: *If this collection sells here, I can finally upgrade my Jeep or maybe even buy Heather a car of her own.*

"Then we have a deal," Rudy said, extending his hand.

Brian clasped it firmly. "Yes, we do."

Brian turned toward the door with his empty case in hand, leaving *Man on a Bench* with Rudy.

"I'll be in touch, Brian. Count on it," Rudy called after him with a parting grin.

Brian strode slowly and confidently toward his Jeep parked around the corner, trying not to break into a skip. Once inside, he let out a howl, then drove straight back to Heather's apartment to share the good news in person. Nobody should get ahead of themselves when making a business deal, whether buying or selling, but Brian was confident he had made the right choice by putting this collection together the way he had and taking it to one of the highest-priced, most exclusive art studios in the entire New York area. Now he needed to get home, tell Heather, and think about his next, or rather, their next, move. Life felt like it was moving forward at warp speed.

When Brian reached the apartment, he found Heather and Flash waiting for him. Heather spotted his smile before he even stepped out of the Jeep, and Flash wagged his tail in anticipation. Brian came inside, dropped onto the couch, and was immediately flanked by Heather on one side and Flash on the other, both waiting for him to tell them how it went at the studio.

"Well?" Heather asked, eyes wide. "How did it go?"

Brian tried to hold back his excitement, but the words tumbled out in one long sentence. "They took my portfolio, Heather! The gallery took it in! And the split, if they sell, is more than fair. It's better than I hoped for!"

Heather threw her arms around him. "Brian, that's amazing!"

Flash barked with his tail thumping against the cushion. That was the frosting on the cake for Brian. He was so thankful to have someone to share the good news with. Still, he cautioned Heather that they couldn't just sit around waiting for a call. They needed to keep moving forward, finding new photo subjects so Brian could build a larger portfolio to take to more galleries. He felt he needed to diversify.

Over the next few weeks, Brian went photo hunting with Flash about three days a week, weather permitting. Heather began looking for a hobby to keep her occupied on the days Brian and Flash were out. She wondered what might come next for them and needed that time to keep her own life balanced.

But the routine didn't last long.

One afternoon, Brian called Heather, out of breath, telling her they needed to meet at the apartment. He had news to share and wanted to tell her in person. As he hurried home, Heather left the hobby shop and went back to wait.

Chapter 18: The Invitation

When Brian and Flash pulled up to the house, Heather was already on the front stoop waiting for them. She had no idea what to expect. This wasn't how Brian usually broke news to her.

Brian jumped out of the Jeep, ushered Heather and Flash inside and quickly shut the door.

"Alright," he said, motioning toward the couch. "Let's sit. I've got something special to share."

Heather gave him a wary look as she settled into her usual spot. "Special? You're making me nervous, Brian."

Flash hopped up beside them, tail wagging.

Brian drew in a breath, then blurted, "The photos I left at the studio… the *Man on a Bench* set… is SOLD! AT FULL PRICE TO ONE PERSON!"

Heather blinked. "Wait… what?"

"Gone! This is a home run!" Brian said as a wide grin spread across his face. "Two weeks, and someone scooped them up."

Heather shot to her feet. "Are you kidding me?"

Flash barked sharply, almost on cue.

Brian jumped onto the couch, pumping his fist in the air. "Hell yeah, he did!"

Heather laughed, throwing her hands over her mouth. "Oh my God, Brian, that's amazing! Who bought them?"

"A man from the Hamptons. Long Island," Brian said, still riding the high. "Apparently, he's a regular client of the studio. Rudy told me he personally called the guy and said, 'Hey, when you're in the area, stop by. I've got something unusual you need to see.'"

Heather leaned forward. "And he actually went?"

"Oh, he went," Brian said. "He walked into the gallery, looked at the piece for maybe two minutes, then he turned to Rudy and said, 'Wrap it up.' It was just like that."

Heather's mouth fell open.

Brian nodded. "And if that wasn't enough, he told Rudy he wanted to meet the photographer in person at his estate in the Hamptons."

Heather stared at him, half in awe, half in disbelief. "Brian... this feels big. Really big."

A few minutes of celebration followed. They hugged each other and laughed while Flash barked like he understood every word. But soon, the laughter ebbed, and the questions began.

Heather tucked her legs beneath her, still grinning but thoughtful.

"Okay… but why does this man want to meet you in person? That's not normal, is it?"

Brian shook his head. "Not for me. When my work sells through a gallery, I never meet the buyer. Ever."

Heather tilted her head as if thinking.

"It has to be a good thing, right? What else could this mean?" Brian asked Heather.

"I really hope so… the question is, what does he want? Just to say hello? To size you up?" Heather speculated.

Brian rubbed his jaw. "Could be. Or maybe he's got something bigger in mind. Some artists get commissioned for projects, events, and even personal collections. Maybe that's what this is."

Heather frowned. "Or maybe he just wants to hang your work on his wall and brag that he knows the artist."

Brian chuckled. "Could be that too. The point is—we don't know. And I wasn't about to agree before talking it over with you."

Heather softened at that. "You bought yourself some time?"

"I told Rudy I needed to check my calendar," Brian said with a small grin. "Then I went to my Jeep, waited about thirty minutes, called Rudy back and asked for more details, including the date, time and address. I also asked if I could bring you and Flash."

Heather arched a brow. "Both of us?"

"Rudy laughed," Brian said. "But he said yes. I told Rudy to let the buyer know the meeting was set. Brian continued, "Rudy then told me the man's name, stressing that the meeting was to be kept strictly confidential and that this man was a very private person."

Heather exchanged a nervous glance with Brian. She didn't press for more details as there weren't any. All Brian and Heather could do now was wait and prepare.

The meeting was scheduled for the following Wednesday evening at 8 PM. There was a gated entrance, but all Brian had to do was buzz for clearance. The dress code was suggested as "comfortable," whatever that meant, and refreshments would be served. That was all the information they had, except for one clear instruction: be on time.

When Wednesday finally arrived, Brian could hardly think of anything else. He and Heather spent the morning tossing around possibilities that may lie ahead. Even deciding what to wear became a challenge. Eventually, Brian suggested they take the day off so they could be well-rested and as relaxed as possible for the meeting that evening. He checked his GPS software to determine when they should leave to arrive on time, or even early, and wait nearby if needed. He also factored in traffic.

At one point, Brian considered renting a nicer, more impressive vehicle than his Jeep, but Heather disagreed. She reminded him that the man was buying art from someone creative, so it wouldn't matter what Brian was driving. Brian agreed.

He estimated it would take about an hour to get to the home, but he decided they would leave a half-hour early. Maybe it was nerves, but he couldn't just sit in the apartment watching the clock on the living room wall.

Brian and Heather snacked on some food and fed Flash as well before they left so they wouldn't arrive on empty stomachs. They had no idea what to expect or what might be served as refreshments once they reached the buyer's home.

They were fifteen minutes early as they approached their destination. Heather had wanted to know the name of the man who purchased Brian's best work, and whose home they were now visiting, but Brian had been sworn to secrecy. Now, as he pulled the car off the road to wait until closer to eight o'clock, he glanced at Heather. She was staring out the window, chewing her lip.

Brian sighed. "You know… maybe it's better if you do know."

Heather turned to him sharply. "You're finally going to tell me?"

He nodded. "The buyer is Daniel Harrington. He's a hedge fund investor. Part-owner of one of New York's local sports teams."

Heather blinked. "Wait! You're serious?"

"Serious," Brian said. "I did some background checking. This guy is mid-fifties, married, and has two grown kids. He also owns another home in Florida."

"Wow," Heather remarked.

For a moment, the car went quiet. Flash gave a soft whine from the back seat, as if reminding them time was slipping by.

Brian knew this wasn't just another gallery sale. Daniel was considered very wealthy, with access to a network of other powerful businessmen like himself. Brian and Heather had never met anyone with this stature before. In preparing themselves, they decided the best approach was to simply be themselves. Daniel hadn't gotten where he was in life by being fooled by people who weren't genuine. The plan was clear: remain calm, polite, let Daniel lead the conversation, and above all, be completely honest.

At exactly 8 PM, Brian pulled into Daniel's driveway and pressed the intercom button as instructed. A man's voice answered, asked who was there, and after Brian identified himself, the gate opened. The long, winding driveway led them past well-lit, beautifully landscaped grounds. Near the front of the home sat two sleek, expensive foreign cars. Brian couldn't help second-guessing his decision not to rent something more impressive than a Jeep for this meeting. But it was too late now as they had arrived. He parked, then turned to Heather and Flash, suggesting they join him as he stepped out and headed toward the front door.

Before Brian could ring the doorbell, the front door opened, and a man greeted them. It was Daniel Harrington, not a butler or maid, but the owner of this large and impressive estate, answering the door himself.

"Good evening, I'm Daniel Harrington. You must be Brian, come on inside," he said.

Brian shook hands with Daniel, introduced Heather and Flash, and followed him through the foyer into a sitting room just off what appeared to be a very large living room.

Daniel was dressed in tan khaki pants, a pastel dress shirt with an open collar, and a sweater. He looked like anyone you might pass on the street; someone no one would guess was a wealthy and powerful man.

A woman soon entered the sitting room and introduced herself as Eileen Harrington, Daniel's wife. She welcomed Brian, Heather, and Flash to their home, immediately remarking on how well-behaved Flash was. He had already settled in the corner of a couch, watching Brian for cues. Brian introduced Heather and Flash to Eileen, just as he had with Daniel, and thanked them both for inviting them into their home.

"Would anyone like something to drink? Coffee, tea… or anything else you prefer?" Eileen asked warmly.

Brian hesitated, careful not to rush. He knew better than to have alcohol since he was driving. Brian responded, "I'm fine for now, thank you."

Heather shook her head politely. "I'm fine for now too, thank you."

Despite the warm welcome, both she and Brian were nervous, doing their best not to show it. Daniel seemed to notice. He turned toward his wife.

"Eileen, I'll have my usual scotch," he said, before glancing back at his guests. "And please, relax. Ask for anything you'd like. Even just water."

Heather gave a small smile. "Actually, a glass of water would be wonderful. Thank you."

When Eileen left the room, Daniel shifted his attention fully to Brian. "I'm very glad you, Heather, and Flash could come tonight," he began. "And let me say this up front—I was genuinely impressed with your *Man on a Bench* piece. I'd love to hear the story behind it. How did you manage to capture that shot?"

The question broke the ice perfectly. Brian leaned forward as the tension in his shoulders eased. "Well, after I graduated from college, I threw myself into photography. At first, I was determined to work only in black and white. I loved the contrast, the depth... but eventually I broadened my thinking. Sometimes color tells the story better, depending on the moment."

Daniel nodded, clearly listening.

Brian continued, "Most of my photos were taken in Central Park. Flash and I go there quite often. You'd be surprised how much life you can capture in ordinary places. The *Man on a Bench* was one of those moments when the timing, the light, and the subject all came together perfectly."

Eileen returned just then, placing Daniel's scotch on a side table near him and handing Heather her water. Brian paused, allowing Daniel the opportunity to continue with more questions or comments he may have.

Instead, Eileen turned to Heather with a pleasant smile. "Would you like to join me in the library? I'd love to show you some of the other pieces Daniel and I have collected."

Heather recognized the cue immediately. This was her moment to step aside and let Brian and Daniel speak privately. She set her glass down. "That sounds interesting. Thank you."

Rising from the couch, she followed Eileen out of the sitting room, leaving Brian and Daniel alone. Flash stayed planted at Brian's feet.

For the next fifteen to thirty minutes, Daniel explained to Brian that he loved his work as a hedge fund manager and that he enjoyed sports, but his secret passion was unusual art. He went on to say that he owned two homes with plenty of wall space, giving him the freedom to fill them as he wished. But when he saw Brian's *Man on a Bench* piece, it sparked a new way of thinking for him. He loved it immediately because it was so fresh and creative, and he wanted to meet the person behind the camera.

Daniel admitted that much of his time was spent making money and mingling with others like himself, but he felt it was time to start thinking about retirement. He was even considering selling his home in the Hamptons and moving to Florida full-time. If he did, the Florida house he currently owns might need to be sold and replaced with something larger and more practical as a permanent residence. That would likely mean having it professionally decorated in a Florida motif.

"Have you ever been to Florida to photograph its sunsets, beaches or palm trees?" Daniel asked Brian.

Brian listened carefully, wondering where this conversation was really headed. Was Daniel hinting at commissioning him to travel to Florida and take photographs specifically for a new home there? If so, how would that be arranged? This was new territory for Brian, and he knew better than to suggest anything too soon before Daniel made himself more direct.

When Daniel finally stopped talking, Brian decided honesty was safest. "I've traveled out west a few times, but never to Florida," he admitted. "And I should say, I've never worked directly for a single client before. So, I'd need to understand exactly what you mean. Are you saying you'd want me working exclusively for you?"

Daniel nodded. "I appreciate your honesty, Brian. That kind of candor tells me I was right about you when I saw the *Man on a Bench*, and again when you walked through the door tonight."

He paused, then continued. "I suggest you, Heather, Eileen, and I take some time to get to know each other better before we talk business. If this does move forward, it'll mean you working closely with me on assignments in Florida. But let's not rush. We've got time."

Eileen and Heather re-entered the room, laughing at something one of them had said, though Brian couldn't quite tell what the joke was.

"So," Eileen asked with a playful smile, "what have you guys been up to? Not getting yourselves into trouble, I hope?"

Daniel and Brian chuckled. "Just talking sports," Daniel said lightly.

Daniel then suggested, "Why don't you and Heather join us for a little tour? You'll get a better idea of some of the other pieces we've collected over the years we've lived here."

Flash trotted close to Brian's side as they walked, never straying more than a step or two away. Eileen led them through a rather large house that did indeed feature a lot of impressive art throughout its well-furnished rooms. The tour ended in the dining room, where Eileen invited Brian and Heather to join Daniel and herself for hors d'oeuvres and a drink so they wouldn't be hungry on their way back into the city. She also set out a bowl of water for Flash, who showed his appreciation by wagging his tail and happily drinking.

Around 10 PM, Daniel suggested it might be time to bring the evening to a close, as he had to get an early start in the morning to close a business deal and didn't want Brian and Heather returning to the city too late.

"It's been a real pleasure meeting you, Brian, Heather and of course, Flash," Daniel said warmly. "Thank you for coming out to our home."

Brian and Heather each shook hands with Daniel and Eileen, smiling. "Thank you both for inviting us," Heather said. "Your home is beautiful, and you've been such generous hosts."

There was a genuine warmth in the room, but Brian sensed it was the right time to leave. As Daniel walked them toward the front door, he turned to Brian with a knowing smile. "You already know how to reach me. I'll be in touch. Perhaps, down the road, we can find a way to work together. Who knows? Maybe I'll commission you for something special."

Brian nodded. "I'd like that."

With goodnights exchanged, Brian, Heather, and Flash climbed into the Jeep. They waved one last time as Daniel and Eileen stood framed in the soft glow of the porch light, before the Jeep rolled slowly down the long, winding driveway, heading back to Heather's apartment.

Both Brian and Heather were too tired to discuss his private conversation with Daniel and agreed to talk about it the next day. Flash was already stretched out on the back seat, worn out from the trip and ready to go home as well.

The next day, Brian gave Heather a summarized version of his conversation with Daniel.

"It's up to him now," he said. "It's entirely possible we may never hear from him again, so I'll just keep working as if last night never happened."

Heather nodded. "That sounds smart."

Flash, stretched comfortably at their feet, had no opinion on the matter—but he was very happy to be home.

Chapter 19: Flash of Memory

Summer came and went without Brian hearing from Daniel Harrington. During that time, Brian and Heather explored areas farther from New York City, looking for two things: photo opportunities for Brian and possible places to live if they ever decided to move out of the city. For now, they were content to stay where they were and save money for the future.

Brian felt he was falling into a rut and not making progress with his photography since selling *Man on a Bench* to Daniel. That one piece had done well financially, but he couldn't seem to match its level of creativity afterward. He feared losing interest in his own goals and ambitions of producing even better work. This fear was the driving force behind getting out of the city to seek new subjects and, perhaps, new inspiration.

One morning, before Brian, Heather, and Flash set out to explore a new area, Heather asked if she could see the neighborhood in Brooklyn where Brian had grown up. The thought had never crossed his mind. He was suddenly reminded that the accident that killed his parents had happened almost three years earlier. After he and Amy sold their childhood home, he had never been back to that area.

As he did every week since she moved to Long Island, Brian called Amy and asked if she wanted to join him and Heather on a drive through their old neighborhood. Her reply was immediate: "No, I don't ever want to go back there again." Obviously, Brian thought Amy had moved on with her life. He couldn't blame her for not wanting to return to see their old home.

Still, Brian believed it might be worthwhile to return to Brooklyn and let Heather see where he had grown up. Perhaps he would find inspiration by returning to a place he had put in his rearview mirror and moved on from. Brian and Heather packed some things for their trip, including food in case they decided to have a picnic somewhere along the way, and made sure Flash had time for a short walk before they all climbed into Brian's Jeep and headed for his old neighborhood.

As Brian drove toward Brooklyn and his childhood home, Heather sat quietly in the passenger seat. Flash was in the back with his window down, head sticking out, taking in the unfamiliar smells, sights, and sounds. He had not been back to the old home since the accident either, and he seemed happy to be in a place Brian had long avoided.

It was a cloudy, cool day, not particularly good for photography, so Brian focused on the drive rather than taking pictures along the way. Suddenly, Flash sat up and barked, startling both Brian and Heather. Brian slowed the Jeep and pulled to the side of the road. When he looked back, he saw Flash with his head fully out the window, agitated. He was panting and began pacing in the back seat, something he had never done before. Brian spoke softly to reassure him, and Flash eventually sat back down, though he kept his head out the window and still looked upset.

Brian resumed driving toward his old home, keeping one eye on the road and the other on Flash in the mirror. Then Flash suddenly stood up again and barked twice. Both Heather and Brian instinctively knew something was wrong. Brian pulled into the next parking lot on the right to get off the road. They were still about five miles from his home, but the area looked familiar to Brian. As Brian glanced to his right, he noticed a cemetery a few hundred yards away. It was the place where his parents, Harold and Ellen Miller, were buried.

How did Flash know? He had only been to that cemetery once in the past three years, yet something about the place seemed to trigger him.

Brian let out a breath. "I've never told you, but this is where my parents are buried," he told Heather. "I haven't been back since the funeral."

Heather turned toward him and brushed his arm. "Then maybe it's time," she said gently.

Brian didn't answer. He simply guided the Jeep into the cemetery lot and turned off the engine. For a moment, he just sat there, realizing he couldn't even remember exactly where the graves were.

They climbed out, Flash leaping down first. Nose to the ground, Flash trotted ahead, weaving through the rows of graves as if he knew where he was going.

Brian and Heather followed in silence until, suddenly, Flash stopped. He lowered himself onto the grass between two headstones, then flopped across them, perfectly still.

Brian froze. "That's them," he whispered. "Mom and Dad."

Brian stared at what he was seeing, while Heather focused on him. All three remained silent for what felt like hours to Brian, though only a few minutes had passed. Heather wrapped her arms around him, and together they sat down beside Flash.

As Brian looked at the headstones, the sadness he had buried so deeply began to rise until he broke down in Heather's arms, sobbing. How could he have never come back? How had he managed to move on? His emotions, raw with grief now, kept him from moving or standing. Flash crawled over and lay his head on Brian's lap, staying there for the next fifteen minutes while the three of them sat in complete silence.

Finally, Brian felt his strength return and managed to stand. He hugged Flash and kissed Heather on the cheek. He found it incredible that Flash had located the cemetery. Maybe it was meant to be?

Brian wanted to leave something on the graves but because he did not know about this unexpected stop he could not leave any flowers. Brian looked around and saw small stones on a few nearby headstones.

He remembered seeing people leave stones in movies, though he never knew why. He found two large stones and placed one on each headstone, touching them lightly as he did so.

He thought of Amy and wondered what it would have been like if she had been in the Jeep when this happened.

Straightening, he brushed the dirt from his hands. "We should go," he said softly. "I promised to show you the old house."

Heather nodded, slipping her hand into his.

As they walked back to the Jeep, Brian glanced at Flash who trotted ahead, tail high, as if eager for the next stop. Brian couldn't help but wonder if he would remember that place too.

They all returned to the Jeep and drove toward Brian's old neighborhood. Brian kept his eyes on the road but also watched Flash, who seemed very aware of his surroundings: alert, not sitting down, watching the houses pass by. When they approached Brian's old home, Flash barked twice. He did remember!

Brian slowed the Jeep and stopped in front of the house, though no one got out. Heather studied the home with interest, trying to imagine Brian's childhood and to find a personal connection to the place. Brian remained silent, while Flash finally sat down, calmer now.

What began as a simple drive to visit an old neighborhood where Brian had grown up had turned into an unexpectedly emotional event, though the feelings were now under control.

Heather glanced at him from the passenger seat. "Why don't we find a spot for a picnic before heading back into the city?"

Brian gave her a small smile, grateful for her gentleness. "Yeah," he said. "That sounds perfect."

Chapter 20: The Settlement

On a day when Brian and Heather had nothing special planned, Brian received an unexpected call from Andrew Forman, the attorney he and Amy had hired to file a lawsuit against the trucking company responsible for their parents' deaths. Brian had nearly forgotten that he and Mike once discussed finding an aggressive accident litigation attorney to pursue the case. Andrew was calling to say he had just heard from the trucking company's attorney and had important news to share.

Although neither the trucking company nor Brian and Amy wanted to go to trial, the case had dragged on for almost three years. The delay came from the insurance company, which refused to meet the settlement amount Andrew demanded on their behalf. With no resolution in sight, the judge had set a trial date, now only days away. Going to court and reliving the memories, pain, and suffering in open proceedings was something Brian and Amy desperately wanted to avoid. Still, they allowed Andrew to keep pressuring opposing counsel representing the trucking firm and the insurance company, making it clear they were prepared to go to court if necessary to secure a fair settlement.

Until Brian's emotions resurfaced during the recent drive with Flash, he had managed to push the accident out of his mind to focus on the present. Amy felt exactly the same way. Now, however, the call from Andrew suggested that the insurance company might finally have met their attorney's financial demands.

A conference call was scheduled for the next day, when Amy, Brian, and Andrew could all be available to discuss the case's current status.

Early that morning, Brian called Amy.

"Are you ready for today?" he asked. "It could go either way… good news if they've finally agreed to a settlement, or bad if we're headed into court."

Amy groaned softly. "Court is the last place I want to be. Sitting there for a week while Andrew presents our case, and then listening to the trucking company's attorney fight back? I don't want to relive all of that."

"I know," Brian admitted. "But we have to be ready, just in case. Andrew warned us their attorney might argue what they believe is a reasonable settlement."

There was a pause before Amy spoke again. "Honestly, Brian, no matter what Andrew's been able to negotiate, I just want to settle. I want to move on."

Brian nodded to himself. "Me too. We'll keep that between us, though. Andrew's fought hard for us, and he deserves the chance to get us the best deal he thinks is possible."

"Agreed," Amy said quietly.

When the conference call began later that day, Andrew opened with the history of the negotiations.

"As you both know," he said, "these negotiations have dragged on for nearly three years. The holdup has been the trucking company's parent corporation. They're out of state, in financial decline, and have already been through lawsuits like yours."

Amy jumped in. "So, the insurance company was just stalling all this time?"

"Partly," Andrew replied. "But the bigger problem is the parent company itself. They're terrified that if they give in too quickly and pay more than they believe is fair in your case, it will set a dangerous precedent."

Brian frowned. "What do you mean by dangerous?"

"If they agree to too much, it could cause real damage," Andrew said with a more serious tone. "They might lose their license to operate in New York. Furthermore, they may even go out of business because another insurance company may not want to insure them going forward. And without insurance coverage, they wouldn't be able to continue operations here or in the three other states where they have subsidiaries. Worst-case scenario, they could even go out of business altogether."

"We don't care what happens to the trucking company," Brian said firmly. "They should pay for what they did."

Amy added, "The driver was fired. The company was already found guilty of negligence even before we filed. They need to be held accountable, and we deserve compensation for what we've been through."

Andrew listened, then replied, "I understand. And I agree with you. But based on the offer currently on the table by the trucking company, and with the trial date approaching, I recommend you settle. This is the highest and best offer I'm going to be able to get on your behalf."

Amy frowned. "How much are we talking about?"

"The settlement is in the low seven figures," Andrew explained. "If we don't go to court now and settle, my fee is one-third. That still leaves a very significant amount to be split evenly between the two of you. You have one day to decide what you want to do and get back to me."

He then continued and emphasized, "If you refuse this settlement and the judge feels the amount may not be reasonable, you'll be going to court next week." He also reminded them, "If we do go to trial, no matter how much the court awards, my fee will increase from one-third of the settlement to forty percent."

Brian replied, "We'll take today to discuss our options and give you our answer tomorrow morning."

"Fair enough," Andrew said. "Call me as soon as you've decided." Then he disconnected from the conference call.

Brian immediately phoned Amy back to discuss the matter. Because he had always taken the lead after their parents' deaths, he wanted Amy to be a full partner in any further decisions about their parents, including this lawsuit.

"So," Brian asked gently, "what do you think? How do you want to proceed?"

Amy didn't hesitate. "Honestly, the settlement amount feels low," she admitted. "But no amount of money will bring them back. And Brian, I don't think I can handle going to court. In fact, I don't think either of us should go through that kind of stress or reopen all those memories."

Brian stayed quiet, letting her continue.

"My recommendation," Amy said firmly, "is that we accept what Andrew fought so hard to get for us, and just move on."

Brian listened carefully to Amy and found himself agreeing with everything she said.

"You're right," he told her. "I agree with you completely. If you want, I'll call Andrew in the morning and tell him we're accepting the settlement. It won't make us wealthy, but it'll make us secure, and I think that's enough."

Amy exhaled, sounding relieved. "Yes. We need to put this lawsuit out of our minds and move on."

Brian said, "The money should be enough to live comfortably for the rest of our lives, as long as we don't spend it foolishly."

"Exactly," Amy replied. "Then it's settled. Call Andrew in the morning and let him know."

They both agreed it was time to shut the door on this chapter of their lives. For Brian in particular, it marked another milestone—one more step toward leaving the past behind and moving forward with his life.

Chapter 21: Four at the Table

Heather and Brian were now financially stable enough to do just about anything they wished. Brian wanted to continue pursuing photography, but he still felt the need to explore other areas for new subject material.

It had been two years since Heather and Brian began dating and eventually moving in together at Heather's apartment. In that time, they had vacationed in Utah and endured a great deal of stress when Flash discovered a dead body at their resort. Brian had started selling his photos in art galleries across New York City, including to one very exclusive art collector, and had also come into a significant financial windfall from the settlement he received after the trucking company accident that killed his parents.

Living in Manhattan had been useful for Brian and a great adventure for Heather, but together they began discussing buying something more permanent, just not in New York City.

Amy continued to stay in touch with Brian and eventually shared that she had been dating a man named Kevin Brady for almost a year. Their relationship had grown from casual to serious. Amy and Kevin had taken a few overnight trips to the western New York mountains and had developed a close bond. After receiving her share of the financial settlement, Amy felt more comfortable moving forward with

Kevin, a vice president at a firm that managed apartments throughout New York. He was mature, good to Amy, and had expressed his desire to "settle down" and start a family with the "right person." They too were discussing buying a home outside New York City if they married.

Amy called Brian one evening and discussed something that hadn't crossed Brian's mind. "I was thinking… how about the four of us, you, and Heather, Kevin and I get together for dinner? It'd be nice to catch up and talk about what everyone has in mind for the future."

Brian smiled into the phone. "That sounds great, Amy. I'm sure Heather would love it too. Where were you thinking?"

"Somewhere quiet but nice in Manhattan," Amy said. "You know, some elegant place where we can really talk."

"Perfect," Brian replied. "I'll talk to Heather tonight. Honestly, it'll be good for us. We've discussed getting together."

When Brian hung up, Heather looked up from the couch. "Who was that?"

"Amy," he said, slipping the phone into his pocket. "She suggested dinner with her and Kevin. Just the four of us."

Heather's face brightened. "I like that idea. It'll be nice to see her, and to finally meet Kevin."

Brian nodded. "Yeah. Amy and I had started to drift apart for a while, but working with Andrew on the case brought us closer again.

This dinner could be good for everyone."

Heather reached for his hand. "Then let's do it. It'll be fun."

"More than fun," Brian responded. "I think it would be a chance to celebrate. After everything that's happened these past couple of years... all the loss, all the changes... we've come a long way."

Heather tilted her head, studying him. "You're right. But look at what's happened since. Your photography turned into something real."

"Feels good to be taken seriously for once," he said, chuckling softly.

"And Amy's moving forward too," Heather added. "She's with Kevin, you're with me... It's like you've both found potential partners along the way."

"Yeah," Brian said as he sat beside her and squeezed her hand gently. "It's about finally having something to be happy about."

During dinner at the restaurant they had chosen in the city, there was laughter and plenty of conversation among the four of them. Over the past couple of years, each had made discoveries about themselves, and now Brian, Heather, Amy, and Kevin felt completely at ease simply enjoying each other's company. Brian and Kevin found plenty to talk about, while Amy and Heather had fun comparing their prospective husbands. It was a lighthearted, enjoyable night.

The dinner lasted longer than anyone had expected because there was such mutual understanding about each other's lives and future plans. Near midnight, they all realized it was time to bring the informal gathering to a close. Before leaving, the group agreed that getting together on a regular basis in the future would be a good idea so none of them drifted apart, and to begin a new and closer relationship with each other.

Brian signaled their server to bring him the bill for dinner. He was the oldest member of the group and could certainly now afford to pay for what had been a great dinner among family and friends. When they left the restaurant, Brian, Amy, Heather, and Kevin shared a group hug and promised each other they would stay in touch. Amy and Heather agreed to be the keepers of the calendar and the group reminders, suggesting they find time each month to meet again.

As they drove back to Heather's apartment, Brian glanced over. "So... what did you think of tonight?"

Heather turned toward him and gave him a soft smile. "Honestly? It was wonderful. Probably something we should've done a long time ago."

"Yeah, I was thinking the same. But tell me, what did you think of Kevin?"

"I really liked him," Heather said. "Down-to-earth, easy to talk to. And I got to know Amy better too. She's stronger than I realized."

Brian nodded, eyes still on the road. "That's good to hear. I wasn't sure how it would feel, all of us together."

"Well," Heather teased, "if I had to rate it, I'd give the whole night five stars." She leaned closer and brushed a kiss against his cheek.

Brian's chest warmed at the simple gesture. He didn't say anything right away, but he knew this was a moment he wanted to hold onto.

Chapter 22: Frames and Futures

While working alone in his makeshift darkroom in Heather's apartment, Brian realized another summer had arrived. He was still selling his photos at a rapid rate in the local art galleries as word spread about his work; however, he never heard back from Daniel Harrington. Brian wanted to pursue something new and unusual, but he had hoped Daniel would contact him and commission him for a special and unique project. Brian felt it would be inappropriate to make the next move, so he continued to wait.

He had also been thinking about the best way to promote the photos he had taken of the old vacant warehouse during the previous autumn, winter, and spring. The photos had been sitting on his desk for weeks, but he still hadn't figured out the best way to market them.

Meanwhile, Heather had stopped traveling with Brian and Flash every day and was working with a real estate agent to find a more permanent home for Brian, Flash, and herself. She had asked the Realtor to help her find something quaint but in good condition somewhere in the Hudson Valley area north of the city. Brian was fine with Heather handling the legwork and told her he'd be ready to see any property she liked.

Amy and Kevin continued dating and had begun discussing the "next steps" in their relationship, though they hadn't yet decided what that might look like. Together, they could afford to buy a very nice home anywhere in the greater New York City area, but they were unsure whether to focus first on marriage or on buying a home.

Amy had moved out of her shared home on Long Island and was now living with Kevin in Manhattan, where he was renting an apartment convenient to his work. She had even made a special trip to meet Kevin's parents separately, since they were divorced.

Brian and Heather were aware of Amy and Kevin's situation but decided the couple should make their own choices without any outside interference or suggestions about how to move forward. Still, the four of them—Brian, Heather, Amy, and Kevin—continued their monthly dinners somewhere in Manhattan to make sure they stayed in touch.

As Brian thought about everything on his mind—his photos, Heather's house-hunting, and Amy's and Kevin's relationship—his eyes went again to the three unique photos of the vacant warehouse. Then it struck him. He decided to take the photos to a good frame shop not far from Heather's apartment.

There, he worked with an experienced framer to properly mat and frame all three photos into one horizontal piece. Though they were in a single frame, each individual photo was triple-matted separately with muted colors that matched the season in which each had been taken.

As Brian watched the framer put the piece together, following his directions carefully, he suddenly realized that this subtle approach, placing all three photos side by side, would most likely make the work much more valuable to a collector. He spent the better part of the afternoon in the shop, and when he finally left with the finished piece of art, he was ecstatic.

He decided to name this piece *Tired, Lonely Warehouse*.

Brian realized he just needed to avoid rushing the process. Framing the three photos of the same subject, taken months apart, had elevated them into something far more striking, a piece of art enhanced simply by the way it was presented.

Driving back to Heather's apartment, Brian could not wait to show her the finished product. They arrived home late that afternoon, and when Heather saw what Brian had done, she let out a scream of excitement, recognizing how much better the three photos looked grouped into one frame. When Heather had first met Brian in Central Park, she wasn't sure what he was doing or how skilled he really was as a photographer. She might not have known then, but she certainly knew it now. Brian not only took great photos but also had a sharp eye for creatively showing off his art.

Brian carefully wrapped this newest creation and called Rudy to schedule an appointment. When Rudy heard Brian's excitement about the warehouse photos, he knew Brian had another winner, something that could make them both a lot of money through his studio. They agreed to meet the next day to discuss the next steps for marketing

Brian's newest photo art creation.

When Brian arrived at Rudy's studio the following day, Rudy was anxiously waiting to see what he had brought to show him. Brian slowly unwrapped the vacant warehouse photos and watched Rudy's expression closely. As soon as Rudy saw the set, framed perfectly to highlight the amazing contrasts and Brian's excellent work, his reaction was one of pure excitement.

"Brian... these are incredible," Rudy said enthusiastically. "Those contrasts... It's brilliant!"

Relieved, Brian sat down across from him. "Glad you think so. Now, the big question is, how do we market this piece? Are you still selling to Daniel Harrington?"

The smile slipped from Rudy's face. He hesitated before speaking. "Brian... Daniel passed away from a heart attack two months ago."

Brian blinked, stunned. "Daniel... died? I had no idea."

"Yes," Rudy said quietly. "And afterward, Eileen sold their estate home in the Hamptons and moved permanently to Florida."

That explained to Brian why he never heard back from him. Brian let out a slow breath, piecing it together.

Rudy leaned forward and said in a quick tone, "Now listen, don't let that stop you. I have another high-end art collector, very serious, who might be extremely interested in these warehouse photos. What I suggest is this: you set the price you feel is appropriate for the piece, and we'll put it under a consignment agreement. I think this could move quickly."

Brian established a price with Rudy, and together they signed the necessary paperwork.

On the way back to Heather's apartment, Brian reflected on the sudden and unexpected death of Daniel Harrington. It was not lost on him that nobody ever knows when something out of the blue is going to change their life, good or bad. He felt both disappointment and sadness upon hearing the news about Daniel. Not because he could no longer sell him any art, but because Daniel had been very kind to Brian and seemed like a genuinely nice person. He considered trying to locate Eileen to express his condolences, but didn't know where to start. He also thought it might look self-serving, so he dropped the idea.

When Brian reached home, Heather was waiting to hear how his meeting with Rudy had gone.

"So, how did it go?" she asked as he and Flash walked in.

Brian set his bag down and sank into a chair. "We went over the piece, agreed on a price, and signed the consignment paperwork. Now it's just a matter of waiting to see if Rudy can find a buyer."

Heather leaned back, curious. "And...?"

Brian hesitated for a moment. "I also learned something sad today.

Daniel Harrington… he passed away a couple of months ago. Heart attack."

Heather's eyes widened. "Oh, Brian… I'm so sorry. I know you two really hit it off when you met."

"Yeah," Brian said quietly. "He was a genuinely kind man. I was looking forward to working with him again."

Trying to shift the focus, Brian asked, "How was your house-hunting day?"

Heather shook her head. "Not successful. I didn't find anything I thought we'd both be happy with. But I don't want to rush it. What's not on the market today could appear tomorrow. My agent said she'd call me if she finds something I might like."

"Sounds like a good approach," Brian said. "No need to force it."

That evening, Brian, Heather, and Flash all enjoyed a quiet night at home. Brian, in particular, could not get Daniel Harrington out of his mind and made sure Heather knew exactly how he felt about her. That led to a conversation about the fact that neither of them had begun the process of putting their estate paperwork together, including powers of attorney and wills. For Brian, that was a sobering but timely thought. He agreed to get in touch with Mike the next day to open the conversation about this topic and also to suggest the same to Amy and Kevin.

During the next few days, nothing particularly exciting or unusual happened. Heather spent time searching the internet for homes for sale in the Hudson Valley area, while Brian continued to clean up his darkroom and wait to hear from Rudy. Flash seemed content to spend a few days at home too. It was late summer, and the weather was very hot. He followed Brian around as usual, but also enjoyed the quiet time in the apartment.

When Mike got back to Brian about putting estate paperwork into place, he suggested Stephen Ross, the same attorney who had handled their estate issues when Harold and Ellen died, should also handle their paperwork. Brian agreed, thinking that should have been his first thought.

"We should meet with Stephen," he said to Heather. "And I think we should call Amy with the same suggestion."

"That's a good idea," Heather agreed. "Whether or not any of us ever get married, we still need someone to speak for us in an emergency, be it a blood relative or best friend."

"Exactly," Brian replied. "It's just too important to leave to chance."

Brian scheduled an appointment for himself and Heather to meet with Stephen. When the day arrived, they sat down with the attorney and went through the paperwork together.

"This is simpler than I expected," Heather remarked, looking over the forms.

"Yeah, clear and straightforward," Brian replied. "I'm glad we finally got this on the books."

By the time they finished, both Brian and Heather felt a sense of relief. The estate paperwork was done, and they were able to check it off their matching to-do lists.

Chapter 23: Success and Reflection

Weeks had passed since Brian had heard from Rudy about the warehouse photo collection, and he was wondering if perhaps he had either misjudged the value as a great art piece or set the sales price too high. That same day, Rudy called, almost on cue.

"Brian, great news! The *Tired, Lonely Warehouse* photos have been sold for full price! I have a check ready for you to pick up at your convenience."

"That's great news, Rudy. I was wondering about the status of those photos just before your call. I'll drive to the studio tomorrow to pick up my check. Thanks for the call!"

Brian passed along the good news to Heather. In retrospect, Brian had graduated from taking only black and white photos with a used camera just a few years before, to now being recognized in the greater New York City area as a really talented, professional photographer. Heather reinforced those exact thoughts to Brian as he left the next day to pick up the check Rudy was holding for him.

"Brian, say hi to Rudy for me. And, by the way, I had all the faith in the world you would not only sell that set, but that you would get what you were asking."

Brian had been on an interesting journey since moving out of his home when he did and was now starting to focus on what his next steps should be, both personally and professionally.

On the way to meet Rudy, Brian received a call from Mike. They had lost a friend from the time they were in college. This was another sudden and unexpected death for Brian. Mike provided the details regarding the funeral as Brian continued to his meeting with Rudy.

After getting paid, depositing the check into the bank and getting home, Brian shared the news with Heather about his and Mike's friend's sudden and unexpected death. Heather saw the look on Brian's face and knew this was another death that occurred too soon and was making Brian more aware each passing day how important every day was.

Heather asked Brian, "Babe, do you want to take a vacation to get away from New York for a while, to just stop trying to find new photo subjects? I hope you don't think you have something to prove to yourself about how good you could become as a professional photographer while still young. In MY humble opinion, you've nothing left to prove to yourself, or anyone else!"

Heather's question caught Brian off guard. He had not considered stopping to take photos even though it certainly was no longer only for the money. He still enjoyed the challenge of finding new ways to express himself through his work. But her question resonated with him just the same.

Brian spent the next few days alone, taking walks, but he did not take a camera with him. He felt Heather had raised a valid question, and it needed to be answered. After thinking about what he wanted to do next, he decided to table it until after he and Mike attended their friend's funeral. During the time they were together, Brian shared Heather's question with Mike and asked him for his opinion.

"What do you think, Mike? Do you think I am trying to prove something to myself or anyone else? I have been working as a professional photographer for a while now, always looking for new and unusual subject matter."

"Brian," Mike responded, "You're the only person who can answer that question. I have what most people would consider a dream job as an attorney. Sure, I make good money, but I worked hard to get a degree to practice law, and I do good work. We all have to do what is best for ourselves. At least until we just can't deal with the potential downside that comes with every profession."

Brian thanked Mike for his quick and candid response. They parted company, promising to stay in touch and not stray from their long-term friendship.

When Brian returned from the funeral, he asked Heather to sit with him so they could discuss together what their future should look like, as a couple. Heather agreed immediately and joined Brian in the family room with two glasses of wine. They talked for hours about how they met, their original ambitions and plans, and where they each were now.

The end result of that evening's conversation produced a conclusion for them both. They agreed to continue to move forward with Heather house hunting and Brian continuing to do what he enjoyed best, looking for unusual and interesting photo subjects to fulfill his love of being a professional photographer. Of course, Flash was always at Brian's side for every new adventure.

Having a close friend like Mike and partners like Heather and Flash helped Brian make important decisions easier. Brian made the decision not to vary from his current routine until and unless something caused him to change what he was doing.

Chapter 24: Combining Business with Pleasure

During that summer, Brian asked Heather if they should combine a trip into upstate New York, somewhere within the Adirondack Mountains, where he could combine work with pleasure and, at the same time, escape an unusually hot summer in the City.

Heather pounced on the idea with a one-word response, "Absolutely!"

She had exhausted her efforts to find a new permanent home in the Hudson Valley, where she had spent a great deal of time searching and felt she and Brian could use some time away. Brian imagined getting some great photos of the scenic woods, waterfalls, and the deep beauty of nature that was calling him to this part of the state, an area where he had never spent any time before. He was also thinking that if he found an unusually interesting area where he could return in the fall and winter, he might be able to recreate a sequence of photos of the same area at different times of the year, much as he had with his warehouse photos.

Brian and Heather began looking in advance of their trip for places to camp. They decided to pack enough clothing, food and water to anticipate any kind of weather, but not take too much. Everything they took needed to fit comfortably into Brian's Jeep. Once they had things figured out, Brian called Amy and let her know he, Heather, and Flash would be headed into northeast New York State for perhaps two weeks camping, that they had stopped the mail, and most importantly, he wanted her to know about this plan in the event they did not have cell phone coverage and could not be reached. Amy indicated she understood and was on board with Brian and Heather, wishing them well and hoping they could have some fun away from the City.

Early the next morning, after squeezing everything they were taking into the Jeep, Brian, Heather and Flash got on the road and headed into the mountains, which were relatively close but would take hours to reach. They had made advance reservations at their first campground to make sure they had somewhere to stay on their first night. After that, they figured they would just play it by ear, so to speak, and see how the trip went.

As expected, including making stops to snack and let Flash out for walks, the first day took almost six hours to get to their first destination. They could have arrived at their first campground sooner but wanted to make sure to take in the beauty of the area as they left New York City and give Flash enough time out of the Jeep as well.

When they arrived at their first campground, it was still light out, and the temperature was almost twenty degrees cooler, which was a bonus. Brian checked into the campground office, and they unpacked for a relaxing evening in the quiet of the area surrounded by woods.

166

The first thing Brian and Heather both noticed was the lack of traffic sounds. There were no loud cars, buses, or beeping horns. The sky was clear, allowing them to gaze at the stars, which they could not see in the city due to the ambient light. Here, there were no streetlights or flashing billboards, just darkness. But they had flashlights and lanterns to assist them find their way around their immediate area. After having a pre-planned dinner, Brian, Heather, and Flash went on a hike in the woods but stayed within approximately one mile of where they had set up their tent. They had been warned that bears could be in any area of the parks and woods that made up the vast area of nature where they were now enjoying nature at its best.

By 10 PM, they needed no coaxing to get comfortable in their sleeping bags and relax, falling asleep almost immediately. Even Flash seemed very happy to be in the woods, but was showing signs he was ready to hit his own bed as well. Early the next morning, a strange sound startled Brian, waking him up immediately. He checked his watch and was shocked that he had slept until almost eight o'clock, later than usual. He quietly slipped out of the tent without waking Heather to investigate the sound, taking Flash, who was already up and waiting to leave the tent.

Brian followed the sound. Then he looked up, high into the tall trees nearby. He saw a beautiful woodpecker doing what woodpeckers do best, pecking into a tree. Brian quickly went back into the tent to retrieve his camera from his backpack and returned to where Flash was still standing perfectly still and quietly watching this strange little bird. Brian adjusted his settings for the early morning light and began taking photos of the woodpecker and then the surrounding area. This is exactly how he pictured the trip into the mountains would be, and he was thrilled. After spending about thirty minutes in the immediate area where he found the woodpecker, Brian and Flash returned to their tent. Heather had awakened but decided not to venture out. She knew Brian had to be nearby and did not want to leave where she was until after they both had returned.

As she was wondering where they were, Brian and Flash emerged from the woods.

"Hey, sleepyhead, where's my hot breakfast, and Flash is hungry too." They joked, got cleaned up and fully dressed, then had breakfast while still enjoying the quiet in the woods. As the sun slowly rose, they packed up again, loaded the Jeep with all their gear and continued their drive deeper into the woods. Brian knew there were lakes and a waterfall not far from their current location. He had hoped to see something really great in that area, which was within an hour of where they had spent the night. Heather and Flash were enjoying the ride as well, with all the windows in the Jeep down so the fresh air could enter and circulate inside the vehicle. This was not something they could do on hot summer days in New York. The heat and fumes from other vehicles would have made it impossible.

Within approximately one hour Brian had reached a clearing along the two-lane road he had been following. Along the way he had only seen one other vehicle going the opposite way. And there was no traffic headed in the same direction which surprised him. He was wondering why more people were not vacationing in these lovely woods during this perfect time of the year, enjoying the cool weather and scenic area.

Suddenly, Brian saw something that made him pull off the road and stop. Actually, two things occurred at the same time. After rounding a bend, Brian saw a small black bear up ahead, crossing the road.

"Heather, look quickly, up the road. Do you see it? There really are bears up here. We're going to have to be careful when we are out of the Jeep."

From that same location, Brian could see a waterfall in the distance when looking past the bear. Brian had hoped to have this type of beautiful and interesting scenery for his photos. Brian turned off the Jeep, then slowly and carefully got out, being as quiet as possible so he would not attract that bear or any of the others in the area. He started taking photos of the waterfall from a distance, not knowing how close he would be able to get to it. Looking at a map, he determined the road they were on would take them closer, so he returned to the Jeep, and they continued forward, but slowly.

Brian was calm from the peaceful environment, but could feel his heart starting to pound harder in anticipation of seeing something special up ahead. Heather turned toward Brian and noticed two things. Brian was intensely focused and smiling at the same time. She smiled but remained quiet so she would not disturb his concentration. In her heart, she knew Brian was truly in his element at that moment. She had not always been right next to him during his previous photo outings, so she felt this was a special moment for them both. Flash remained quiet but focused while in the back seat with his head out of the window, sniffing the air and panting. He, too, seemed very happy to be in an unfamiliar environment.

After driving for about another thirty minutes, Brian reached a picnic area just off the side of the road. The waterfall was now in clear sight and close enough to photograph. He pulled over and parked so they all could get out and stretch. He also wanted to determine if he had any "clean" shots worth taking of the waterfall from where he was.

Brian stood on one of the picnic tables, steadied himself, aimed and fired. The sun was shining, and there was moisture coming from the waterfall, which created a beautiful rainbow. He had an opportunity for some perfect photos.

He began to wonder if this was somewhere he should consider returning during a different time of the year to try to replicate the photos he had just taken. He took out a notepad and jotted down where he believed they were based on where they had spent the night, and then the time it took to get to this location. He also used a device he had in his backpack to provide him with his exact coordinates to help him return here.

When Brian turned around, he saw both Heather and Flash watching him in complete silence, with Flash sitting quietly and Heather beaming. Both Heather and Flash seemed to instinctively know Brian was in heaven. Brian smiled back and spoke for the first time in several minutes, keeping his voice low.

"I think I found the next big opportunity. And you guys have witnessed history. When I'm famous for getting great photos of this waterfall during different times of the year, you can say you saw me do it!"

As Brian said those words to Heather, Flash stood up and barked, wagging his tail. No, they were not in danger. He seemed to be in agreement. Heather and Brian broke out laughing, then all three got back into the Jeep and continued on their journey.

Chapter 25: News, News and More News

Brian, Heather, and Flash spent two more days in the area near the waterfall, with Brian continuing to look for photo subjects. They began each day with breakfast, cleaned up their campsite, and slowly moved on and off the road, driving and walking through the beautiful, wooded area of this magnificent place they had found. They stopped for lunch each day to rest and make sure everyone was getting food, and that Flash in particular had enough water. The cooler weather and trees provided shade, which was a special break for them all from the harsh, hot New York City summers.

Finally, Brian and Heather agreed it was time to head back home. Brian had taken several photos which he believed would be more than acceptable for him to sell in the local galleries back in New York, and they needed to move on to other matters. Amy had called and said that when they got back, they should all get together to talk about some things going on in her life. It was not urgent, but she sounded excited.

The first thing Brian did after they got home, unpacked, and cleaned up was call Amy.

"Hey, kiddo, what's up?"

"Hi, Brian. Why don't you, Heather, Kevin, and I get together at one of our favorite pizza restaurants in the City? We've always enjoyed their food, but they've never seemed too busy to take care of us while providing their usual good service. That would give us a chance to all get caught up."

Brian agreed and said he would talk to Heather and confirm with a return call later that day. They all agreed to meet the following Saturday night for dinner.

After everyone arrived and ordered food, Brian turned to Amy.

"Okay, Amy, you called this meeting. While we wait for our pizza, why don't you bring us up to date with your news?"

Amy and Kevin smiled, looking at each other before Amy turned back to Brian and Heather,

"Okay, well, Kevin and I have two items to tell you about. You guys know Kevin and I have been house hunting for a few months now, and guess what? We found a home we fell in love with that is located in the Hudson Valley area, just outside Courtland. We decided to make an offer to buy it, and while you guys were camping in the woods, we received word that our offer was accepted. So, we are going to become the owners of this fabulous home of our dreams!"

Brian and Heather each stood and hugged Amy and Kevin while ordering another round of beer to go around the table. When the server brought them their drinks, Brian stood and gave a toast.

"Congratulations to Amy and Kevin for being on the verge of becoming first-time home buyers! Heather and I wish you all the joy you deserve, and hope all goes well as you move forward toward taking ownership of your new home!"

Brian and Heather had a lot of detailed questions about where it was and why they had decided to purchase this particular home. They spoke about the home that was to become Kevin's and Amy's in about a month, for perhaps an hour, when Brian realized Amy was still grinning and staring at Kevin. Brian put up his hand to get everyone's attention at their table to stop the conversation. Then he looked at Amy and reminded her she had indicated there were two items of news, but they had only talked about the new home they are buying. Brian sat back, folded his arms, smiling back at Amy and asked what the other big news was.

Amy and Kevin, while still grinning and looking at each other, turned back at the same time toward Brian and Heather. Amy blurted out, "Keven asked me to marry him, and I said yes! We're going to get married!"

That brought another standing ovation from Brian and Heather, and more hugs all around. Laughing ensued, which came with tears of joy coming from Amy's and Heather's eyes, while Brian and Kevin shook hands and hugged. During the following few minutes, it was impossible to understand who was asking what questions or answering them because they were all talking rapidly at the same time. Finally,

Brian put up his hand again.

I suggest we go around the table, one at a time, to get all the news sorted out. Buying a home and getting married is a big deal. I would like to make sure both of you, Amy and Kevin, have an opportunity to provide all the details to Heather and me.

For the next hour, the four happiest people on the planet spent time going back and forth with questions and answers about Amy's and Kevin's new home and their wedding plans. The home took second place behind when and where the wedding would occur, and all the details about that topic. Amy became the spokesperson for Kevin and herself while explaining that she and Kevin had decided to keep their wedding small, low-key, and in Courtland after they had moved into their new home. Then, with grace and the smooth movement of a pocket thief, Amy suddenly reached into her pocket and produced the engagement ring Kevin had given to Amy when he proposed.

"You buried the lead," shouted Brian, which started another standing round of hugs. Amy proudly showed Heather the ring first, and then another round of beer was ordered. Brian was starting to wonder if they would all be taking Uber rides home from the pizza restaurant.

Then came the biggest news of the evening. Amy asked Heather to be her bridesmaid, followed by Kevin turning to Brian, asking if he would be Kevin's best man. The servers at the pizza restaurant had to wonder what was now going on at the table where Brian, Heather, Kevin, and Amy had been seated because this last bit of news set off another round of joy, accompanied by hugs, more tears of joy, and one heck of a celebration.

When they all sat back down, Brian and Heather each gave another toast to Amy and Kevin and jointly accepted to serve in the wedding party as requested. Brian, Heather, Amy, and Kevin had been getting closer, but this certainly was a time to celebrate so much good news all at once. They continued to talk about timing and details, more about the wedding plan than the new home, which at first was the big news of the night but now had become second to the wedding. Amy and Kevin had decided to get married fairly quickly, as this was still summer, but they wanted to marry in the fall when the leaves were changing color in the Hudson Valley area. They had located a small party venue as their location and decided to be married by a judge who was a friend of a friend living in Courtland and who had been referred to Amy and Kevin to conduct the wedding ceremony. They had also spoken to mutual friends who would assist with photography.

Amy made it clear to Brian that she did not want him to take that personally, but wanted Brian to be able to enjoy himself as a member of the wedding party and not feel responsible for taking the wedding photos. Brian expressed that he had no objections. A florist had been contacted, and the date was down to one of two Saturdays in mid to late October. Brian was thinking to himself that is when he had wanted to return to the woods to get his next set of photos of the waterfall for his photo collection, but remained silent, knowing he would figure out how to do both, get his photos in the mountains, and be in Amy's wedding.

Finally, as it became close to midnight, a decision was made to call for Uber rides home. Nobody wanted to make the mistake of driving after having consumed that much beer. Brian paid for the pizza and drinks, which was followed by a group hug. Heather and Amy made plans to speak during the coming week and go over all the wedding details again to make sure they had everything covered. Then they all headed toward the door of the restaurant to leave.

Suddenly, a very loud "Congratulations!" came from the staff in the restaurant as everyone walked out through the front door. That was the icing on the cake, or pizza and beer in this case.

Brian's and Heather's car arrived about the same time as Kevin's and Amy's. They hugged goodnight and parted, then each headed home. On the way to Heather's apartment, Brian turned to Heather, who seemed very far away in thought.

"Hey, you, a penny for your thoughts."

Heather turned back toward Brian and told him, "I haven't had an opportunity to get to know Amy very well and did not yet know Kevin well either. My instincts are good, both about their decision to buy the home they have selected and that they seemed to be on the same page about everything else in life as well. I saw the smiles, the mutual respect Amy and Kevin had for each other, and simply felt they had a good chance of making things work out together in their futures."

"You're right. I agree that they both seem like they are on the same page about a lot of things, and you picked up on that."

Brian was also remembering the days when he and Amy were younger, and he was getting flashbacks of both the good days and the bad, and realizing that with his little sister buying a home and getting married perhaps both he and their parents had instilled all the right things into Amy's core beliefs in life to help her make the decisions she was now making.

As the car continued to Heather's apartment, Brian sat back in his seat, folded his arms, and found himself not only in deep thought about the news he had received that evening, but also feeling content and happy for Amy.

Heather was watching Brian, deep in thought and smiling. She felt she could read his mind. She took his hand, leaned over and kissed him on the cheek, whispering, "Good job, big brother."

Chapter 26: To Have and to Hold

Following the historic and eventful evening out together, Brian, Heather, Amy and Kevin each went about doing what they had been doing prior to the big reveal about Kevin's and Amy's new home purchase, their engagement and wedding plans, and with Heather and Amy planning the wedding details together. Kevin continued to work where he was an executive with an apartment management company, and Brian continued to plan and find photo opportunities with Flash. Kevin and Amy closed on their home just outside of Courland and set up housekeeping in something other than an apartment together for the first time. They met neighbors and began to live a life with Kevin commuting into New York City and back every day, and Amy worked toward furnishing their new home, wondering what she should do to keep busy in their new community.

Fall approached, the wedding date had been set for the second Saturday in October, and Brian began planning a trip back to the Adirondack Mountains. But he wanted to only take Flash and find the exact same location he found during the summer. This trip was all about the waterfall, which he wanted to photograph in summer, fall and winter. Heather was on board with his trip, understanding this was a work mission and would have a much shorter duration in terms of them being separated. Brian decided to go during the week following the wedding, as it would be colorful, and weekdays would present fewer cars on the road with fewer tourists looking at the beauty of the area.

As Amy's and Kevin's wedding day approached, all four members of the wedding party rehearsed their parts and responsibilities. In addition, Brian was pre-packing for a quick getaway the Monday following the wedding. Amy and Kevin had chosen a perfect setting, sent invitations to a limited number of guests, which included friends from Brooklyn, college, and where she had worked in the Manhattan department store. Kevin invited some of the closest friends he had made at work, along with his mother and his father, each of whom had been dating since their divorce. He also invited some college friends. Amy's and Kevin's wedding guest list, which was intended to be small, had grown to about 50 people. The wedding photographer and florist confirmed they would honor their commitments, and all was set.

Amy and Kevin were in agreement to forgo a bachelor's party for Keven and a bachelorette's party for Amy the night before the wedding. They each wanted to put all of their energy into planning a wedding that would be meaningful and memorable instead. When the second Saturday in October arrived, Amy, Heather, Kevin and Brian all felt ready and spent a quiet day together at Amy's and Kevin's home. This was a day of small talk, bonding, dealing with wedding day jitters, and just relaxing until later in the day. The wedding was set for 5 PM.

But an hour earlier, all four were dressed and ready to go to the party venue where the wedding had been planned to take place. Brian had even washed the Jeep that morning.

During their time at the venue, just before the wedding, Brian met with Kevin privately and offered him support, permanent friendship and his sincere best wishes for a happy life with his sister Amy, reminding him that if Kevin broke her heart, Brian would kill him. They both shook hands, had a laugh, hugged, and got ready for the ceremony. Heather was in a separate room with Amy, offering sisterly love, support for her and quiet time to reassure Amy that all would go well. Guys do guy things. Women, of course, are always more mature.

At the appointed time, music that had been recorded on the sound system owned by the venue began to play signaling to the guests to take their seats. A few minutes later, Kevin and Brian each walked down the aisle toward the judge who was waiting patiently under a trellis covered in white flowers. Heather then took the same walk, finally followed by Amy, dressed in a beautiful modern white wedding dress. When they had all reached the trellis, each took their respective positions, the music stopped, and the judge began with his opening remarks.

Brian listened carefully to the advice the judge was giving to Kevin and Amy, thinking they probably would not remember much of what was being said. His own mind was on his parents, Harold and Ellen, wondering what their wedding day was like. He struggled to keep his own focus. When the time came for Kevin and Amy to exchange vows, they both did so flawlessly. And with that, Amy was now Amy Brady. They kissed, turned, and smiling broadly walked to the back of the room from where they had started down the aisle, but now as a married couple. Everyone in attendance smiled, waved, and took pictures. A modest reception was waiting for all in another room, which everyone seemed to find without any difficulty.

The reception was the last item on Kevin's and Amy's list of things they needed to plan, and the only item where they had different views. Kevin had wanted a more formal dinner, but Amy insisted a buffet with a variety of food would suffice. They could afford the more formal dinner, but Amy also was thinking of her parents who had lived a modest life in Brooklyn, and even though she never told Heather or Brian about her reason for only offering a buffet it was about how she was raised, in a modest home by humble middle class people who she felt may not approve if they were alive.

That evening, following toasts by Brian and Heather, a first dance by Kevin and Amy, then dancing and mingling with guests for about an hour, Kevin and Amy stopped the party. They cut a traditional wedding cake, which was then shared with the guests, and announced they were off on a secret honeymoon that absolutely nobody knew about. As a courtesy, they had told Heather and Brian they were flying to Florida for a week but leaving the next morning, not directly from the wedding.

Guests began to leave; however, Amy, Kevin, Heather and Brian remained to the end and said goodnight to everyone who had come to the wedding. Then the four sat down at a table in a corner of the room that had been reserved just for them. Brian offered another toast and then told Kevin and Amy he felt as if he represented his entire family, including his deceased parents, wishing Amy and Kevin a beautiful life together and one that would last forever. He felt himself becoming emotional but recovered in time to walk over to Amy and give her a tight hug, with his eyes tearing up. He turned to Kevin and shook hands, offering him support as well. Heather followed Brian's lead with hugs to both Amy and Kevin and some whispers into their ears. Then it was time for Brian, Heather, Kevin and Amy to head to their respective homes as the evening had officially come to a close. The music had stopped, the photographer had left, and even the judge was nowhere in sight.

This was the end of a chapter in Amy's life as a single person, and the beginning of a new one as a life partner with another person.

Brian and Heather left first so Amy and Kevin could be the last ones to leave the venue and start their married lives together.

When Brian and Heather got home, they both remained quiet and in deep reflection for a long time before finally calling it a day and going to bed. But there is no question what was on both Brian's and Heather's minds when they put their heads on their pillows that night...

Chapter 27: Another Trip to the Waterfall

On the Monday following Any's and Kevin's wedding, while they were enjoying their honeymoon in Florida, Brian was on his way with Flash to the mountains where he would try to find the waterfall that was waiting for him. Along his drive, Brian turned on some upbeat music to take his mind off Saturday, when he watched his sister leave the nest in a way more important than just moving out of the home where they had grown up, or into a home with a boyfriend. She was now married and would be starting a family of her own. Brian pictured himself as Uncle Brian to her children, and a close brother-in-law and friend with Kevin as they got older.

Although Brian was focused on his driving, his mind was definitely somewhere else. Flash, however, had his head out of the window as they continued north toward the beautiful and colorful area ahead. Flash seemed to be able to sense the change in smells, and maybe Brian was imagining it, but as he looked toward Flash and Flash looked back at Brian, they seemed in sync, and both sensed where they were going would be as beautiful as a postcard.

Brian stopped for lunch and got Flash out of the Jeep so he could walk around, get water, and get a brief rest from the drive. It was Brian's hope that he could get to the area near the waterfall with a brief overnight stay after they were already well into the mountains. He wanted the opportunity to take photos in different lighting while remaining in that one spot for several hours, knowing this would take perfect timing and patience, but he was determined to make it work. If he got the right shots on this trip, he would want to return in a few months when all the beautiful leaves that were currently on the trees were gone. With luck, there would be snow on the ground, and he might have another award-winning set of photos that would not only sell for a significant price in the right art studio but perhaps make him famous. He could feel his heartbeat increase as he was driving and thinking about the importance and possibilities of this one event.

It was getting dark when Brian and Flash approached the campsite in the woods where Brian had planned to stay, and he was very glad to see it. He had driven all day, starting before daybreak, and was very tired. He pulled off the road and set up camp. Brian fed Flash, but he was too tired to eat much himself. Within minutes, both Brian and Flash, tired from the drive that day, had fallen into a deep sleep.

Brian had an alarm set to wake him just before daybreak the next morning so he and Flash could eat and head immediately to the coordinates he had saved in his GPS. It only took Brian about an hour to arrive where he wanted to be, and just as he exited the Jeep, the sun began to rise. He fed Flash but skipped breakfast for himself, picked up his camera and walked immediately to the special spot where he could perfectly see the waterfall in the early morning light.

There was dew on the grass, and it was much cooler than when they had been there during the summer. He set up his tripod for these shots, something he did not always do. He was also preplanning his photos, trying to make sure he would take photos of the changing light that was starting to shine on the waterfall.

Suddenly, because there was some mist in the air, a rainbow appeared over the waterfall, and Brian was ready. He was shooting through a canopy of maple, elm, and oak trees, framing the waterfall in all its glory, probably like nobody had ever seen it. Brian was trying to take deep breaths to slow his heartbeat and remain steady as he aimed his camera at his target, taking photo after photo and after photo. Flash remained seated next to him, silent and watching Brian work. He was a perfect match for his partner, not moving or making a sound. Not even a squirrel would be able to get his attention while Brian was taking photos.

Within two hours, the sun had risen high enough in the sky to reduce what was an exceptional view of the waterfall to something still beautiful, but it wasn't the same. Brian was so pleased that he had pushed himself to get to the waterfall early and capture what could possibly be the best photos he had ever taken, even better than the *Man on the Bench* photo. Brian suddenly realized he was starving. He stopped taking photos and made some coffee over a campfire. He made sure Flash had an opportunity to take a walk and also get water. Brian was considering driving around the area to look for other areas of interest and return to this spot for some sunset photos, but realized the direction of the sun would be wrong, and he also realized he was dead tired.

After about another half-hour to make sure Flash was ready to go, Brian packed, got back into the Jeep, turned around and headed for home. He was positive he had done the very best he was going to do that day and wanted to get back home to Heather. Brian and Flash slowly drove out of the woods and said goodbye until winter.

It took longer to get back into the City than it took to get to the woods the day before. It felt like they had been gone longer than one day, but Brian realized his adrenaline had pushed him to get to his coordinates without feeling any pain or fatigue on the way. That is what he was feeling now. He was a lot more tired, and so was Flash, who had his head inside the window and was lying down on the seat, dozing off. Brian called Heather to let her know his status.

"Hi, I'm just checking in to let you know I made it safely to the waterfall last night, and this morning I got some great shots!"

"That sounds great, but you sound tired. Are you okay to drive?"

"Yeah, I'm tired, but fine and I can't wait to see you when I get home."

They had previously agreed that, because she would not know if Brian would be taking photos if she called him, she would not call.

And, unless there was an issue, he would only call when he and Flash were on their way back. Heather was glad to hear from Brian and could hear both the excitement and fatigue in his voice while he explained how the trip had gone. He mentioned he would be home later than originally planned and was driving the speed limit because he was very tired and wanted to be extra careful. He suggested Heather not wait up, but he would be home that night.

When Brian and Flash reached Heather's apartment, Brian removed all the gear he had in the Jeep and, as quietly as possible, entered the apartment. To his surprise, the lights were on, and Heather was sitting up reading a book while waiting for Brian and Flash to arrive home. Brian got the hug he needed, and Heather had one for Flash, who expressed happiness to see her as well.

"You have to be exhausted. Why don't you wait to put everything away tomorrow and come to bed?"

Brian agreed and also knew he would have to wait until the next morning to be awake enough to check out all of his photos properly.

When morning came and Brian awoke, Heather was making breakfast for him. Flash had already eaten and even gone for a short walk with Heather. Brian could not believe he had slept so late. He was anxious to eat, have coffee and get to his camera. When he was able to get to the photos he had taken of the waterfall, he could not believe his eyes. They were perfect! If anything, they were even better than he believed he had. He shared the photos with Heather. Brian knew this was only the second of three events for this set of photos at the waterfall, and he would be returning in the winter. So, he decided to relax, put everything away and take the day off. He also decided to just spend the day with Heather and Flash in a nearby park and not think about taking photos. He needed to clear his head. And wait for it to snow!

Chapter 28: Will There Be a New Home?

During the coming weeks, Brian and Heather both decided to take some time off. Brian wanted a break from looking for special photo targets and taking those photos, and Heather had grown tired of house hunting. She was not feeling successful in finding a home she could present to Brian as a great new residence for them to buy.

As winter approached, Brian was seeing ads on television for year-end car sales events offering special pricing. They certainly could afford to upgrade from Brian's Jeep and needed to be prepared for Heather to be able to get around better if they moved out of the City into the Hudson Valley area. Brian felt certain that day was coming soon.

Brian began searching on the internet for a new vehicle but quickly narrowed down what he believed he still needed. Another utility vehicle with four-wheel drive. After going to a few dealerships and driving various makes and models, he decided to buy another Jeep, but this time he would buy a larger and more luxurious model that came equipped with more upgrades than he had. He made the decision to trade in his Jeep Wrangler for a more upscale model. He also selected a gray metallic model that had four-wheel drive and a lot of new technology he did not have in his little black Jeep.

Heather was not exactly thrilled with the thought of having such a masculine-looking vehicle for herself, so when Brian took possession of his new Jeep, they went shopping for her vehicle. Many people live their entire lives in New York City and never own a vehicle. Both Heather and Brian suspected they would find a home outside the area where they could not manage without a vehicle for Heather to shop for groceries and run other essential errands. Heather was going to need something other than Uber.

After repeating the steps to research a vehicle for Heather, but with her more personally involved, Brian and Heather settled on a German-made SUV, which included four-wheel drive and looked much more civilized, at least to Heather. If they were going to live in the suburbs where their neighbors were driving upscale foreign vehicles, they felt they should make an effort to fit in better. They had some concerns that some people might think they do not belong there. This entire experience gave Heather and Brian something to do together that was practical in nature and fun.

At approximately the same time Heather and Brian had settled on a vehicle for Heather, they received a call from their real estate agent. A home that fit the description Heather told the agent they were looking for had just come on the market, and because the owners were going through a corporate relocation, they were motivated to sell. Brian and Heather asked to see the home the next day and scheduled a showing.

The home in question was not far from where Amy and Kevin had purchased a home, located on the outskirts of Courtland, a popular area of the Hudson Valley. This area is considered to be a suburb of and not far from New York City.

When they arrived at the showing the next day, Heather and Brian were blown away. The home they were about to see was considered part of Courtland, but it was located on a two-acre lot and set back from the roadway in a heavily wooded area that was absolutely beautiful. Heather had become accustomed to city apartment living, so if they purchased this very modern home in such a remote area, it was going to require some adjustments. Brian and Heather both realized this was going to be a much different living environment, but the adjustments were all positive. The real estate agent suggested once again that this home sounded exactly like what Heather had said she and Brian would want, and it was priced to sell quickly.

Brian decided to take Flash for a ride to see this home when he went to see it with Heather as he did not want to leave Flash alone in the apartment. When Flash exited the new Jeep Brian was driving, Flash seemed disoriented for a moment, then slowly and carefully began to explore all the lush landscaping that surrounded the home, sniffing as he went. The real estate agent was watching this and asked Brian and Heather if their dog had to approve of the home for them to make an offer. She asked that with a straight face, but was really joking. Brian immediately responded to her.

"Good catch on your part. If Flash does not like this home, we're leaving."

After a few awkward moments, Brian and Heather started laughing and told the agent to relax. It was just Flash being Flash, and they all needed to go through the entire home to determine if they believed this home would be a good fit for the three of them, and perhaps some additions to their family in the future.

Their tour took about forty-five minutes to walk through the home, and while Heather spoke to the agent, Brian and Flash went through the home a second time. Brian was memorizing the floor plan and thinking about what he needed to know before they went any further with an offer. Brian caught up with Heather and the agent and began asking about everything he could think of so he would be a better-informed buyer and owner.

The agent arrived prepared with a list of features and details about the home and gave it to Brian so when he returned home with Heather to discuss this home, they could compare what they each saw to their expectations. Brian wanted to make sure both he and Heather were on the same page before they got back to the agent and either created an offer or told her they needed to keep looking. There was no pressure from the agent, and none was needed. Brian was overwhelmed with everything he had seen, even though his only comparison had been the much older and smaller home where he and Amy had grown up in Brooklyn, which was not a fair comparison at all.

Heather shook hands with the agent, saying they would be in touch. Then Brian, Heather, and Flash drove into Courland to make sure they would find that area acceptable to them for the many years ahead that they expected to live there. Following a drive around and through Courtland that included the surrounding area, they proceeded back to Heather's apartment to have their first serious discussion about the purchase of this home, the first good candidate from the time Heather first began her search many weeks earlier. During the drive back into the city, Brian gestured to Heather.

"Take a good look at this area, Heather. It's beautiful here. I expect this area gets more snow than we have experienced living in New York City. It will be beautiful at first, then more difficult when driving. And, unlike living in the City, we are going to have a front row seat to enjoy all four seasons. And I see people of all ages driving around here. All the vehicles I've seen have had younger couples, some with small children in their cars. But there are grandparents here, too. And almost all the vehicles I am seeing are foreign utility vehicles, much like what you have now."

"Brian, it is no wonder you are such a great photographer. You have amazing powers of observation! I was looking around too, but you are seeing things I didn't. And, by the way, I loved the house. It looked like it could be featured in House Beautiful!"

"Yeah, I didn't want to say too much while we were there, but I agree completely. And that lot, with all those trees! I think we'd love living in this area, and I think we'd love the house for a long time too."

"Brian, I was doing the math while we were walking through the house. We've lived frugally for a long time, saving money in addition to the funds we've both received from other sources. Let's make an offer when we get home, okay?" Brian gave a short response.

"I agree completely."

When they reached home, Heather called the agent and said she and Brian had enough time to make a decision while driving home and told the agent she and Brian were ready to make an offer. Heather verbally communicated Brian's and Heather's offer and asked the agent to send them the offer paperwork for them to sign and forward to the seller's listing agent.

That evening, Heather called Amy and broke the news.

"Hey, kiddo, we have some news for you. Brian and I just made an offer on a home that is about five miles from where you and Kevin live."

"Are you kidding? That's fantastic!" Amy yelled to Brian, who was in his home office,

"Hey, Kevin, Brian, and Heather are going to be neighbors!"

"Hold on, Amy, we just made an offer. Let's not get too far ahead of ourselves, okay?"

Heather felt she had to calm Amy down and explained that nothing was a done deal, and it was too early to start the celebration. She just wanted to share the good news now because even though it was still too early to tell her parents in Boston, she had to tell someone.

After Heather's call to their agent, Brian found himself pacing around in Heather's apartment, jotting down all the things he had not asked and did not see on the features and benefits sheet that the agent had provided. He wondered about the source of water and did not ask if the home had public access to sewer or if it was on a septic system. Heather sat silent in amazement that Brian even had these questions on his mind. She and Brian had not discussed what any home they purchased should or should not have, which also included gas in addition to electricity. Suddenly, they were both making notes in preparation for a second call to their agent to verify what they either knew or thought they should know, and also what the home did not have that perhaps they would have wanted.

Heather called the agent back and went over all the questions on Brian's and her lists. The agent knew the answers to all of the questions, and it was all good news. The agent said she had just sent the offer to Brian and Amy electronically for their respective signatures, and when she received it back, she said she would forward it to the listing agent.

That night, while both Brian and Heather were trying to relax, the home was the only topic of conversation. They had just purchased two new vehicles and thought that was a big deal, but this was totally unexpected, and they were moving very quickly. Brian had the photos that came with the listing, but he had taken some photos of his own when they did their walk-through of the home. He also decided to call his insurance agent in the morning and inquire about the cost to insure this home, and ask what else he needed to know. They were not concerned about being able to afford the purchase or the upkeep, but Brian was now thinking about the many things on their respective lists that had not been discussed.

As they prepared for bed, Heather leaned over and gave Brian a huge, tight hug.

"Brian, I can't thank you enough for everything you have been doing for us. I have a new car. You have been so supportive about buying a home and have put so much thought into where we should live, and your feedback about the house today was great. When we first met in Central Park a few years ago, I sensed you were a good man and someone I could trust. I am getting to watch you do things that Amy has already seen as your sister. You're smart, kind, and careful about the decisions you make for yourself and anyone else those decisions may impact. You make me so happy!"

Brian was propped up on their bed just listening. Heather had provided positive feedback to him in the past, but he just took it for granted as something a close friend and possible future wife would say. While he listened, he decided he had to add one more item to his follow-up list the next day and then start shopping for an engagement ring. But he did not speak. When they were too tired to talk anymore about the home, they both fell fast asleep in each other's arms and did not wake up until the sun came up the next morning.

Chapter 29: Big News, More Planning

The next day, while waiting for their cell phones to ring with a call from their real estate agent, Brian turned to Heather.

"I know I told you this, but regardless of the outcome of our offer, I need to start planning one more return trip into the mountains to capture the waterfall with snow on the ground and bare trees so I can complete the three photo groupings I have been planning for months."

That did the trick. Heather received a call from the agent who congratulated Heather and Brian on receiving an accepted offer. The sellers were impressed with the fact that Brian and Heather were decisive and felt comfortable enough to move forward with an offer to the seller that they could not turn down. Because Thanksgiving was a week away, both the sellers and buyers wanted to close before Christmas if possible, something they were each now telling their respective agents. That would take some hustle, but the wheels were put into motion to make it happen.

Heather called Amy again, this time with better news.

"Amy, if we can get to a closing without any complications, we would be in our new home in time to host the Christmas and New Year holidays with you and Kevin as their first guests!"

Amy's response on the other end of the call went up an octave.

"Heather, that is great news!"

Kevin then called Brian,

"Hey, Brian, Amy just told me the good news about your offer on the home you guys wanted to buy. This is fantastic news, and welcome to the neighborhood."

When Brian and Heather each ended their calls, they each started new to-do lists that covered packing, moving and other details with smiles and high fives all around.

The next call from Heather needed to go to her parents in Boston with the good news about their soon-to-be new home. Both Robert and Doris were home when Heather made the call and told them to put her on speaker so they could hear some news together.

"Mom, Dad, our offer was accepted on the house we really, really liked! And there's more. Brian's photo art is selling, Brian finally bought a newer, bigger Jeep, and then we went out, and I got an SUV too. We are going to need newer and better cars to get around out of New York, and we need 4-wheel drive for snow in the winter."

All of this news was a bit overwhelming for Robert and Doris, but they accepted it with joy and approval. Doris presented a question to Heather,

"Honey, when will you and Brian be able to move into your new home?"

"Mom, if everything goes right, we will be in our home for the holidays!"

Heather remained on the telephone for an hour answering questions from her parents while Brian sat silently with Flash at his feet. Brian fully realized that this was all very big news to Heather's parents and could not help wondering how his own parents would take all this in if they were still alive and living in Brooklyn.

Brian motioned to Heather to put the call on hold for a moment so he could ask her a question. Heather asked her parents to hold for a minute. She had no idea what Brian was about to bring up, but she was prepared for just about anything at this point.

"Babe, do you think it would be too forward to ask if Robert and Doris would like company for Thanksgiving?"

Somehow, with everything else going on, there had not been any discussion among the four of them about who may or may not have plans for the coming holiday, which was now just a week away. Heather was partially stunned and totally embarrassed that she had not had that conversation prior to now with her own parents. She also wondered why they had not invited Brian and Heather to come up to Boston for that holiday. She felt a bit awkward about asking, but presented Brian's question to Robert and Doris.

"Hey, we have another idea. Would you two like some company for Thanksgiving? We know that's just a week away, but we would love to see you again!" This time, Robert spoke, "Honey, thank you for asking, that would be a wonderful idea. Your mother and I would love to see you. We had considered asking the same question over the past few weeks, but we didn't want to impose or put any pressure on Brian to make a second trip to see us."

They all quickly agreed that the trip to Boston the following week was on, with Brian smiling and nodding while Heather told her parents to expect to see them in Boston the following week.

"Sorry, we should have asked you sooner, but we've been just a bit busy and distracted lately."

Details about dates of arrival and departure were discussed, and then the call was completed.

A lot of information had just been communicated in a very short period of time, some of it planned, some not. But Heather turned to Brian and thanked him again for saving the day.

"You know, you can be amazing sometimes. I really had not thought about trying to get to Boston for Thanksgiving. I have been focused on getting into our new home in time for the holidays, and I am a bit embarrassed about the fact that I wasn't thinking about being in Boston for Thanksgiving. Thank you!"

"Should I put on my magic cape now or wait until later?"

Both Brian and Heather began laughing so hard they had tears running down their cheeks. Brian got a hug and a kiss on the cheek from Heather. He was glad he had thought about going to Boston while listening to Heather talking to her parents, and he just felt they should try to get together for Thanksgiving.

This was a truly eventful morning that would leave both Brian and Heather feeling good about it for the entire day.

Chapter 30: Ring, Ring!

As soon as they were off the call Heather decided to check each other's to-do lists and make sure they were on the same track with the trip to Boston, packing for their move, and actually moving from Heather's apartment to their new home in Courtland.

Brian reminded Heather, "Remember, very soon after we move, I want to get back to the mountains to that last waterfall photo."

"I'm totally aware of your plan to go back to the mountains. But we need to stay on track, organizing what we have at my apartment to determine what should go to the house in Courtland. We need to pack everything that we will want to take with us as soon as possible."

"I agree. Why don't we go room by room and take inventory?"

Heather agreed, and at the end of completing that task, which took only a few minutes, Heather told Brian, "Now that we have completed that, I need to run a few errands and will only be gone for about an hour."

"I don't have a problem with that, and I want to run a few short errands myself."

They both left, with Brian taking Flash along with him.

Brian had not yet shopped for an engagement ring for Heather, and it struck him during Heather's call with her parents that he had better take the next step, and soon. They had just purchased cars, were in the process of buying a home together and were visiting Heather's parents in a week. He could not think of a better time to make their relationship more permanent, but needed to move fast.

Brian drove to a highly respected jeweler who owned a jewelry store in Manhattan, not far from Heather's apartment only about twenty minutes away. When Brian entered the store, he introduced himself to the owner and explained why he was there.

"Hi, I'm Brian Miller. I'm on a mission. And, this is Flash. I hope he can come in. I need an engagement ring, and your store came highly recommended to me."

"Hi, Brian. I'm the owner, Simon Stein. Thanks for coming in, and Flash is welcome too. If you don't mind, I have several questions for you before we continue. Are you considering a traditional diamond ring or something else? And do you have any knowledge about diamonds?"

"I am thinking about buying the woman I want to marry a traditional diamond ring, and yes, I have some knowledge about the four C's, cut, color, clarity and carat weight, right."

Simon was impressed with Brian's understanding of diamonds, so he moved Brian toward a glass case where some of the most popular types of diamond rings were on display. Brian began to look at the wide array of diamond rings with all the diamonds different in cut, design and size, and then suddenly stopped.

Brian looked up at Simon and raised a sudden concern about selecting a ring for Heather instead of allowing Heather to select her own ring. Simon agreed that that was a great question.

He told Brian, "About one-half of my buyers surprised their girlfriends with rings, and the other half let their girlfriend select their own rings."

Brian then looked up at Simon again and asked, "So, how many rings were returned that had been a surprise?"

Simon answered under his breath, "Too many."

Brian thanked Simon for his candid response and said he would be returning with Heather, the woman he planned to marry, soon. They shook hands, and Brian signaled to Flash that they needed to go.

Seeing the wide range of band colors, styles, sizes, and shapes of the diamond rings at the store brought Brian to his senses. He should have known better about trying to surprise Heather with a ring. He had seen a lot of movies where a man surprises his true love with a ring, and she just automatically loves it forever. Simon's response about returns meant Brian would need to come back with Heather so she could select what she wanted for herself. Brian made one other stop on the way home, and then, after getting there, stayed silent about where he had gone and why.

After dinner, Brian cleared the dishes and asked if he and Heather could have a conversation about one more important topic for that day. They moved to Heather's couch and Brian confessed where he had gone earlier, and why he came home empty-handed. Heather sat there in shock, tears of joy streaming down her face. Not only was Brian the guy she really wanted to marry, but this was just one more reason. His consideration of others, in this case, allowing Heather to select her own engagement ring!

They had some dessert and coffee while discussing Heather's preferences in rings based on her own knowledge of that topic and the fact that she knew some women in her life who were wearing a ring that had been presented as a surprise. But several friends had said what they received would not have been their first choice.

The following morning, Brian, Heather and Flash headed back to the jewelry store to see Simon. When they entered the store, Simon put away something he had been working on so he could greet them.

"Hi again, Simon, this is Heather. We are going to need your assistance."

"Hi Heather, you're getting married to one smart boy here."

It only took a few minutes for Heather to make the decision about her ring. She chose a one-carat traditional ring with a silver band. It was simple, elegant and perfect in her opinion. And it fit! Brian presented his credit card and asked Simon to "wrap it up." It was one thing to select something this important in a store, but another to know how it was presented. Brian was pretty sure, even though the ring would not be a surprise, Heather would not mind waiting for a proper proposal in a different setting, perhaps during a dinner out that evening.

When they were on the way home, there was practically no conversation between Brian and Heather in Brian's Jeep. Flash sat on the back seat, looking back and forth between Brian and Heather, and then back at Brian. He may not understand English, but something was different, very different. Finally, Brian turned to Heather and, as if they had just been out shopping for a lamp, calmly asked, "Heather, would you like to go out to dinner this evening, perhaps somewhere a little more upscale. We may need to dress up a bit more than usual, and there may even be music."

Heather, blushing and laughing at the same time, said, "Sure, why not? A girl needs a nice night out every once in a while!"

Brian and Heather went to an upscale Italian restaurant that had dimmed lighting, a mood suitable for romance, and soft music playing in the background. Brian had called ahead and made reservations, not taking any chances that they would not get a good table. He also let the restaurant know this was a special occasion dinner. After they arrived and were seated, Brian ordered a bottle of wine that he knew was one of Heather's favorites. They took their time ordering, discussing small talk about their new home and other matters that were not that important, considering they both knew exactly why they were there that evening.

Finally, dinner had been served, consumed, and dessert was ordered. When it arrived and the server had walked away, neither Brian nor Heather picked up a spoon to taste their ice cream (they both ordered ice cream, but in different flavors. Heather sat still, smiling at Brian and saying nothing. Brian smiled back, then spoke first.

"Would you be terribly upset if I told you I forgot to bring the ring?"

Heather was stunned at first, but concentrated on not losing her composure. Before she could respond, Brian reached into his pocket and pulled out a small box with Heather's ring inside. Brian, grinning broadly, just chuckled and, while opening the box that revealed Heather's ring inside, presented it to Heather, asking, "Heather Parker, will you marry me?"

Suddenly, the staff who had been watching went silent.

"Why, of course, I will, Brian Miller!" Heather answered.

Brian placed Heather's engagement ring, the one she had selected, on her left hand ring finger while the staff broke their silence and began clapping. The owner of the restaurant was fully prepared and suddenly appeared with a small, rich chocolate cake that had one lit candle sticking out of the top.

The owner leaned down while placing the cake between Brian and Heather, thanking them for making his restaurant a part of one of the most important events in Brian's and Heather's lives. He then picked up the dinner check, which the server had already placed near Brian's right elbow.

"Please, allow me to pay for your dinner and selecting my restaurant for your special occasion. It is my hope that this is only the first of many good things to come your way, as you are obviously meant for each other. I know, because I am a very good judge of character and I am rarely wrong about people."

Heather and Brian stood, shook hands with the restaurant owner, and thanked him for their complimentary dinner promising to return soon. Brian and Heather gave each other a hug and of course kissed to seal the deal. Brian requested that the cake be wrapped to go and apologized for the melting ice cream that remained on the table. Then, without another word, they headed for the door to retrieve their car from the valet and head home.

Brian and Heather were quiet during the ride back to Heather's apartment, but Brian was mentally congratulating himself for having the sense to fall in love with Heather, suggesting she select her own ring and, of course, ask her to marry him. This was a huge moment for them both, so they both knew calls to family and friends would need to be made when they got home or the next day.

But, for now, they just rode in silence, enjoying the quiet and the ride home, lost in their own thoughts.

Chapter 31: Thanksgiving in Boston

The next week, Brian, Heather, and Flash took Heather's new car for their trip to Boston, the Wednesday before Thanksgiving. The ride was uneventful, and even though this day is always reported to be one of the busiest travel days of the year, they had no issues getting to Robert's and Doris's home exactly when they had planned. They were tired from their trip, but Robert and Doris were very excited to see Brian and Heather, and wanted to spend time getting updated about everything, the new home, any wedding plans (there were none at this point), and of course, the engagement ring was the center of attention.

When they arrived, Doris was waiting for them at the front door and immediately went out to greet Brian, Heather, and Flash.

"Oh, my, look at this lovely new car! And, how we have missed seeing all of you!"

"Hi, Mom," responded Amy. "We can't wait to come in, have time with you and dad, and enjoy this very special holiday as a family!"

Thanksgiving Day was spent with Robert and Brian catching up and talking about things they wanted to talk about, while Heather and Doris wanted to spend time alone to talk about what mothers and daughters discuss when the daughter is about to buy a home with her fiancé, and then plan a wedding.

By the time dinner was served, everyone was all caught up with each other's lives, so dinner talk was kept light and was focused on what was on Robert's and Doris's minds, while Brian and Heather remained mostly silent and just kept smiling. Brian was acutely aware that both he and Heather had done the right thing by coming to Boston to be with Heather's parents for Thanksgiving, but his mind was on his parents, moving to the new home, and getting that last waterfall photo. He remained the quietest person at the dinner table, which was suddenly sensed by Heather.

She turned to Brian and asked, "Are you as tired as you look?"

Before he could respond, Doris commented, "I just realized how much you both must have on your minds. We are so thankful that you would take time from your busy schedules to make the drive to Boston and back to be with Robert and me for Thanksgiving. It would be completely alright if you wanted to get back to New York tomorrow."

Heather looked at Brian for a response, but remained silent. Brian put down his dessert spoon and, after a brief pause, turned to Doris and Robert.

"I wouldn't have wanted to be anywhere else this Thanksgiving Day. But you're right, Doris, maybe Heather and I should leave tomorrow morning as you just suggested. Traffic is going to be a bear, and we really do have a lot of items on our checklists to complete. But

213

just so there is no misunderstanding, this trip was a great idea, and we appreciate your hospitality. Being with family is really important to both of us."

Friday came with Brian, Heather, and Flash on their way back to New York. It was a good visit. A very, very good visit.

Chapter 32: The Big Move

After the Boston trip was in the books, both Brian and Heather began a rapid-fire exercise to make sure everything that was required of them by their Realtor to get to a real estate settlement as soon as possible was completed and returned to her. Brian had their new home inspected. He and Heather teamed up to make the necessary changes with the utility companies. They made sure they had property insurance in place for the new home when it was time to move. And they worked through moving furniture and personal items around in the apartment, including items that would be boxed for the move. Movers were contacted and their quotes were received. Brian and Heather narrowed their selection to one company.

For two people who had not done this as a team in the past it was like watching a ballet, perfectly choreographed with nothing missing from their respective checklists. The week before the settlement had been scheduled everything went into warp speed with respect to scheduling the walkthrough of their new home which had now been vacated by the sellers. They made sure they were still on the movers' schedule, and had their addresses changed at the post office. Everyone who buys a home and moves goes through this, but there is only one first time, and neither Brian nor Heather wanted to miss anything that would get in the way of their plan. Each night, at the end of the day, while still going through all the planning and execution of their upcoming move, they ended the day exhausted and went to bed earlier than normal.

In addition to all of the items they had checked off their lists, they decided to leave the least important item last, shopping for some additional furniture to help fill their new home which was much larger than any apartment where either Brian or Heather had lived. Each of them was silently thinking about when they were growing up, and remembering how much their respective parents had in their homes. They knew they needed to fill some space, but decided not to buy furniture just to fill a room with something if it didn't have a purpose.

They spent a few days, when there was spare time, shopping for what they considered essential, but added some things that had been on a "someday wish list" for a new home. It was another act in their ballet they were performing, agreeing almost immediately on what they both liked and felt was needed in their new home, and disregarding what they agreed could and should wait.

In the evenings, this is what Heather thought about the most. She had dated but never met someone quite like Brian. He seemed to be on the same frequency with her about everything they were doing together, even before they moved, and more importantly, before they had even discussed their future, getting married, and having a family. She had allowed those topics to slide because she felt completely comfortable that when the time came to have those other discussions, everything would work out.

Finally, everything was in place for their move. The home inspection came back to Brian and Heather with no issues. A property insurance binder was in place. Funds were in escrow. Paperwork had been signed. The movers were on standby. It was now time for a final walkthrough of their new home with their real estate agent because the next day, which was just four days before Christmas, was moving day.

The walkthrough went as planned. Brian and Heather sealed up the last boxes for the movers who were coming the next day, immediately after the settlement, and then Brian and Heather would be taking the next big step in their respective lives, moving into their new home together. Brian and Heather spoke with Amy and Kevin to keep them up to date with their progress and make plans to get together for both Christmas and New Year's Eve. Amy and Kevin had suggested that Brian and Heather should actually join them at their home for Christmas to allow Brian and Heather to unpack and get moved in. That now made sense and became the new plan.

Settlement day came without issues, the movers came on time, and with that, Brian and Heather, along with the movers (and of course, Flash), moved to their new home in Cortland. Heather and Brian followed the moving van in their own vehicles with Flash riding with Brian. After arriving at their new home the job of unpacking and getting moved in was next. By this time Brian and Heather were truly exhausted and ordered a pizza delivery for their first night in their new home. They laughed about how cheap that seemed, but it was also practical. They could have gone out to dinner somewhere but felt a need to stay close to home that first night. They needed to get lamps and clocks plugged in. They did not have to be married to act like a couple that had been together for several years, which in reality was not the case. The ballet they were in was now in Act Three, and it just felt normal to them both.

Heather and Brian spent the next couple of days working together quickly and efficiently to unpack and put things away. Neither of them appreciated clutter and both liked living in an organized space. With that came the chore of figuring out where everything should go in the kitchen and other rooms. But the kitchen was definitely taking center stage as it was the one room in the home where they both needed to agree; they would each naturally go looking for things like plates and glassware. And, how should the silverware should be placed? There was mostly agreement, but for the first time, there was some serious disagreement about a few of these details.

Without warning, and for the first time, Brian and Heather were not totally in agreement. Each had lived alone and set up housekeeping for themselves in the past. When Brian moved in with Heather, he did not try to change where Heather had everything placed in her apartment; he just moved in and added some personal things of his own to hers. Should this have popped up in either Brian's or Heather's minds, that not agreeing with everything may be just the start of how people live together in a new environment and learn how and when to give in to their soulmate? That question did not enter either Brian's or Heather's minds as they managed to settle their differences to get to the end of this task and get completely moved in.

When Christmas Eve Day arrived, Brian and Heather had achieved their common goal of having all their furniture in place. Artwork and photos hung on the walls. And, they both knew where everything was in the kitchen. In the late afternoon, they called Heather and Amy to check in and to say they were on the way to dinner and were starved.

"Hey, Amy, we have done it! We are in, we have unpacked, and we are on the way. Wait, I think Brian and Flash are already in the car!"

"That sounds about right," Amy laughed. "Men!"

Brian and Heather were totally exhausted, both physically and mentally. Heather had taken care of dealing with her landlord, closing out her lease and returning the keys the day before. It was official. Brian and Heather had done it. They purchased a home, became engaged, and were now living together in a home that they both loved. It was time to take a beat and start to enjoy this new stage of their lives together.

Chapter 33: Christmas Cheer And Checklists

The drive to Amy's and Kevin's home on Christmas Day took only a few minutes, as it was just a few miles away in a subdivision filled with beautiful homes much like one would expect to find in this part of the Hudson Valley. The original plan had been to get together on Christmas Eve, but that was changed when Amy suggested Brian and Heather might want to spend their first Christmas Eve together in their new home.

After Brian and Heather arrived and were given a tour of Amy's and Kevin's home, Brian and Kevin gravitated to Kevin's home office while Heather and Amy moved to a sitting room between the kitchen and family room. Dinner was in the oven, so they all had about thirty minutes to connect and relax.

Kevin began their conversation by asking Brian a few questions about his new home.

"So, Brian, what are you doing for snow removal for your driveway and sidewalk? Have you hired someone to handle your landscaping yet? Are you and Heather meeting any new neighbors?"

Brian sat in total silence. None of these items was on his checklist, and he was certain they did not exist on Heather's either. Kevin started to laugh while waiting what seemed like hours, watching the color drain from Brian's face.

"So, you thought you had everything figured out, eh?"

Brian looked back at Kevin and put his head into his hands.

"Kevin, I guess I totally forgot about a few details in my moving plan. I feel like an idiot."

"Why don't you and Heather check out the neighborhood social media groups. You guys should join a few and introduce yourselves as new to the neighborhood and ask for assistance with snow removal, lawn care, and also find out if there are any community events you both should know about."

"Yeah, I think you're right about that. I've got to mention all your suggestions to Heather and then follow up as soon as we get past the holidays. Thanks for bringing all this up. Being a first-time homeowner is totally new to me."

Heather and Amy were having a similar conversation in the sitting room. Then it was time for dinner to be served, so they decided to continue talking during dinner about the details they did not have time for now. How Brian and Heather needed to maintain their new home became the main topic of conversation over dinner.

As Amy served dinner, Kevin stood up, glass of wine in hand. Looking at Brian and Heather, he began a toast.

"I think it is only appropriate to salute Brian and Heather for all they have achieved in such a short time, but mostly for having the good sense to move so close to Amy and me."

There were laughs, and more wine bottles were opened during Kevin's toast. Brian needed that drink and appreciated Kevin's sincere welcome to him and to Heather.

"Amy and Kevin, Heather, and I want to thank you for your hospitality. But I think we need to eat now before I chew off a finger because I'm starving."

As the wine was poured for Kevin's toast, Heather noticed Amy had something different in her glass that looked like apple juice. Brian had not seen what each person was drinking, nor did he care.

Dinner was followed by dessert, and then all four moved into the family room, which was perfectly decorated and ready for company. There was more small talk about what Brian, Heather, Kevin, and Amy had all been doing over the past several weeks and what everyone had planned for the coming year.

Heather raised her hand to speak. "Remember, New Year's Eve will be at OUR new home. I just wanted to get that in before we all had any more to drink."

The wine continued to pour during dessert, but Heather noticed that only Amy was not drinking. Brian yawned and looked at Heather.

"Babe, maybe it's time we head back home. You look tired. I know I am. Flash looks like he's ready to go too, because when I stood up a minute ago, he went to the front door signaling he wanted to go out." Everyone hugged, Brian and Heather thanked Kevin and Amy for their generous hospitality, and all said goodnight.

On the way back to their new home, there was no conversation in the car. Flash was lying on the back seat while Brian and Heather were each deep into their own thoughts. This was not normal, but it did not necessarily indicate that something was wrong. A lot of events occurred in Brian's and Heather's lives during the past couple of months, and both were visibly tired.

As they reached their home, Brian stopped the car at the foot of the driveway and just sat, looking toward their home, which seemed a long way away.

Heather turned to Brian.

"Hey, is something wrong?"

Brian turned back to Heather. "No, but I was just thinking it's a good thing Kevin asked me about snow removal and landscaping because somehow I just hadn't even thought about those things."

Nothing in Brian's previous experience would have triggered those items to be put on his checklist until it was too late to set up. He was also taking in the beauty of their home at night from a distance, with the lights turned on, waiting for them to come home. Heather put her hand on Brian's shoulder.

"Brian, give yourself a break! We've done a lot of new things together for the first time, and if snow removal and landscaping are the biggest problems yet to be solved, we're just lucky."

With that, they parked the car in the garage, headed inside, and directly to bed. The next day would bring a new day and more follow-up that needed to be addressed.

Chapter 34: New Year and Big News

On the days between Christmas and the New Year, Brian spent time in his home office reorganizing the art he had hung after they moved in, replacing it with what he believed were some of his best photos that he never tried to sell. He asked Heather to look for and join what she believed were the best local social media groups and start introducing them to their neighbors, mentioning their need for snow removal, landscaping vendors, and basically begin finding people who they believe could become not only resources, but perhaps friends. This had been something missing in their lives, and now they were starting a new chapter.

"We shouldn't be hermits. We need to develop new friendships where we now live!"

"I couldn't agree more!" Heather began following up, while still unboxing a few things she had not had time to address before Christmas.

Brian found himself creating a new checklist that included the items he asked Heather to follow up, but he also felt he needed to try to schedule the things he had said he would do after they moved into their new home. Mostly, he started watching weather forecasts in the mountains in an effort to determine when he should return to get that last the waterfall photo. He needed to complete that one piece which contained three photos of the same subject taken during summer, fall, and winter. It was an itch he needed to scratch. Brian also began thinking about how he would move forward in the coming year and even further out, wondering what he wanted to do for the rest of his life. He did not have any solid plans for what he would do or where he would go to pursue new subject matter after he completed the waterfall photos.

Heather had similar thoughts on her mind as she worked through a revised and updated to-do list, which now included Brian's request to help them find friends in the Courtland area. She was also wondering whether to mention to Brian that she noticed Amy was avoiding wine during Christmas dinner. That could have meant she was pregnant, but wondered if that was true, why had Amy not mentioned it to either Brian or herself. And she felt something had changed a bit between Brian and herself after they completed their move. It was almost as if they had completed a goal and had nothing meaningful more to pursue together.

She assumed two things to clear her head. Amy and Kevin would reveal if she was pregnant when they were ready and second, if it seemed like the bloom was off the rose between Brian and herself, maybe they were both just tired, in a new environment with new checklists, and it meant nothing more.

Still, she could not help wondering, now that they were engaged, who should bring up a wedding date and other details that go with becoming Mr. and Mrs. Brian Miller. She decided to put that last thought off as well. The timing did not seem right, and she wasn't overly concerned about the fact that Brian had not mentioned it.

By the time New Year's Eve approached, Brian and Heather had made significant progress with their respective checklists. They had a snow removal vendor Brian was able to hire to get rid of snow if and when it came over the coming days, and he had hired a landscape company that would take care of their needs with the lawn, trees, and shrubs on their two acres of land. They were in winter now, but neither Brian nor Heather wanted to wait to find someone to begin making sure their little estate home looked good without the need to start looking for help during the coming spring. Brian had another thought.

"Hey Heather, do you think we need to get in touch with Amy and Kevin to make sure we're all set and on the same page when they arrive for New Year's Eve at the new Miller home?"

"Brian, the menu is set, and everything needed for an intimate but important party in our new home has been purchased. We're ready to host Kevin and Amy with the same type of warm reception that was shown to us on Christmas. Quit worrying!"

As New Year's Eve approached, Heather suggested she and Brian call her parents in Boston. Brian immediately agreed, and Heather made the call.

"Hi, Mom, Brian, and I wanted to wish you and Dad a Happy New Year!"

Of course, Robert and Doris were happy as usual to hear from Heather and Brian and be brought up to date on news about how happy Heather and Brian were in their new home. During that call, Brian found his mind wandering again, thinking about his parents. He found the longer they were gone from his life, the more he missed them.

New Year's Eve arrived, and so did Amy and Kevin. This was indeed a huge moment for Brian in particular. With great pride, he walked Amy and Kevin through their large and newly updated home. His heart swelled with pride while showing Kevin and Amy what they had achieved and received praise and kind remarks from both Kevin and Amy upon making this dream come true.

Heather, in particular, felt very proud of her hard work helping to find a welcome and suitable home for Brian and herself, and the comments from Amy and Kevin helped her satisfy any question in her mind that she and Brian had found exactly the right place to call home for a very long time in their futures together.

When appetizers were served and both the red and white wine were offered along with beer, scotch, bourbon, and the vodka Brian had thought to put into his mini bar Heather, Kevin, and Brian each selected something to nosh on and something from the bar to go with it. Except Amy quietly took Heather into the kitchen and asked if she had any juice in the refrigerator, like apple, tomato, or even Coke or Pepsi.

Heather had everything Amy had requested and more and suggested she select what she wanted. She showed Amy how their icemaker worked in the refrigerator and then asked if Amy would like anything else. Amy just shook her head, stayed silent, selected some apple juice from the refrigerator, and began to walk back toward the family room to join Kevin and Brian. Heather took Amy by the arm and pulled her aside.

"Is there something you would like to share with me or with Brian and me?"

Amy looked at Amy, starting to blush, then whispered, "Yep, ya got me. I'm pregnant. I'm sorry I haven't said anything yet, but Kevin and I wanted to wait a bit longer to make sure I was far enough along to say something."

Heather grinned, gave Amy a big hug, and promised to keep her secret from Brian if she wanted.

"Heather, maybe that would be a mistake. You guys are my family, and I already suggested to Kevin that we should let you and Brian know a baby is on the way. I don't like keeping secrets and knew we couldn't wait much longer with this news."

When Amy and Heather entered the family room, Amy decided to let Brian know what she had just told Heather.

"So, Brian and Kevin, have you two guys solved all the problems in the world yet, or are you ready for some other type of conversation from the women in your lives?"

Both Brian and Kevin looked up with interest, and Brian taking the challenge.

"You go, girl, ya got something important to share with us?"

Amy looked at Kevin and said, "She figured it out!"

Kevin nodded and said, "Go ahead, let it fly!"

Brian was now completely confused and hoped that bad news was not coming. He put his drink down, then looked at Heather for a signal. When he did not receive any sign from Heather, he turned back to Amy and said, "Amy, you have the floor."

Amy walked over to stand next to Kevin, who was comfortably seated on a couch and enjoying the moment. She then turned back toward Brian and Heather and blurted out, "We're pregnant!"

Brian leapt to his feet and rushed to give his sister a big hug with tears of joy streaming down his face. The pent-up emotion of missing his family, the fatigue of the move, the checklists, and everything else that had been on his mind melted away to address this very important moment in his life. He wanted Amy to know how happy he was for her and for Kevin.

Then he turned and shook hands with Kevin and suggested a special toast was in order. Everyone refreshed their respective glasses, and Brian gave a loving and powerful toast from his heart about how it was so important to him to be a part of a growing family again. He spoke for almost ten minutes when Heather caught his eye and, with a tilt of her head and a smile, but not needing to speak, sent a silent message that Brian probably said all that needed to be said and that they probably should move to the dining room for dinner. Brian and Heather were still on the same page and could communicate without speaking.

Brian got the message, hugged both Amy and Kevin again, and said, "Let's eat!"

The announcement from Amy definitely changed the tone from just a New Year's Eve party to a celebration of greater importance. They all took turns talking during dinner and dessert about the timing of Amy's and Kevin's announcement and how they all should be looking forward to a great year ahead. Brian took the time to also say he felt blessed to be in this place at this time with the people in the home he and Heather had purchased, suggesting this was one of the best moments in his life.

As the evening came to a close, Heather did her best to repeat Brian's toast and comments during dinner. Once again, as Amy and

Kevin were preparing to leave to go back to their own home, Heather could not help but wonder if getting married was even in Brian's mind somewhere, and if it was, why he had not discussed it with her. If it wasn't, why not?

After Amy and Kevin left, Heather and Brian cleaned up the dishes but stayed mostly silent, deep in their own respective thoughts. The new year was upon them. Each was wondering what was next. But they headed for bed without saying much more.

Chapter 35: One More Waterfall Photo, and a New Idea

A few weeks into January, Brian saw what he needed regarding the predicted snow in the mountains.

"Heather, the conditions are perfect. I need to make plans to return to the waterfall.

"I understand completely. Do you want to make this last trip alone like you did in the fall?

"Actually, I do."

Brian needed to concentrate on his driving due to the winter conditions. He also needed more time to think about some other things that had been on his mind lately, particularly since New Year's Day.

When Brian and Flash headed for the mountains, they left even earlier than they did the last time. Brian was determined to get as far as he could as fast as he safely could to complete this mission. Along the way, he began thinking about this trip and how to handle the waterfall photos grouping assuming he would be successful in getting some great photos of this third but vital piece of this subject. He remembered, while driving in silence, something his father had once told him. Sometimes, one plus one equals three.

He started wondering if he should actually not sell the waterfall photos. Perhaps he should try to buy back the *Man on a Bench* photo art that had been purchased by Daniel Harrington when he and his wife Eileen still lived in the Hamptons and before his sudden heart attack. He knew Eileen had sold their Hamptons home, and she was living in Florida, but he wondered if he could convince her to sell that photo group back to him, for a profit. He was also wondering about the same thing about the *Tired, Lonely Warehouse* photos. In his mind Brian was wondering if this was the right time in his life to do something different with his work to help create a new and different image of himself and his work that would set himself apart from all the other photographers trying to find buyers in a small and unique space of professional photographers, not only in the greater New York area, but everywhere.

Brian arrived very late at night, where he and Flash had camped previously, with the waterfall not far away. There was snow on the ground, the leaves were gone from the trees, and it was cold. Was he going to get what he wanted from this trip? Would anyone understand how taking photos of the same subject at different times of the year was not just a warehouse or just a waterfall, but truly unique art?

Early the next morning Brian and Flash took their walks and had breakfast while it was still dark. After going to the location where he had taken the previous photos Brian set up his tripod and aimed his camera at the waterfall, waiting for sunrise. He was not disappointed.

As the sun rose, that waterfall and the surrounding area came to life in his eyes and in his head. He could picture how the three final photos would appear when they were matted and framed together, grouped in one frame. He took several photos, changing the settings on his camera in an effort to give himself the best opportunity for this one last photo that could make or break his idea. This special set of photos would be considered art. These photos were more difficult to take than his *Man on a Bench* photo. And it was also different from the warehouse grouping, which some may see as a more natural way of showing the same subject during different times of the year.

Flash let out a loud yawn and a whine, indicating they had been in one place for a long time. Brian laughed to himself. Flash had a better sense of timing than Brian. He had been taking photos for almost two hours and had not moved from the same spot. It was time to wrap things up and head back to Courtland. Brian and Flash had been in the snow for this photo shoot for a long time. Both were cold and hungry. Brian put his camera and tripod away, broke camp and then, inside his Jeep, he and Flash both ate what Brian had brought for lunch on this trip. Flash seemed very happy to be back inside a heated vehicle and after eating flopped down on his seat and dozed off. It was time to go home.

As they pulled away from the waterfall area, Brian called Heather.

"Good morning, sleepyhead. I am just calling to let you know my mission to get the last waterfall photo has been accomplished, and I am headed home.

"Brian, are you happy with his effort to capture what he wanted?"

Brian hesitated for a moment. "I'm not only happy with the photo shoot, but I also have a new idea I'll share with you when I get home. This trip to the mountains helped me clear my mind and create a new idea with regard to what I want to do next with my photos."

That piqued Heather's interest. "Drive safely home. I'll have a special dinner waiting for you when you get here."

In his mind, while driving back to Courtland, Brian was reviewing the photos he had just taken. Flash napped. Brian was still thinking about trying to buy back both the *Tired, Lonely Warehouse* photos and the *Man on a Bench* art piece he had sold. He felt that if he could combine the *Tired, Lonely Warehouse* grouping, the *Man on a Bench,* and *The Waterfall* groupings, he may be able to create a newer and broader image of himself, not just a New York area professional photographer.

After he reached home and had finished the wonderful home-cooked dinner Heather had ready and waiting for him, he asked her to join him in their family room so he could explain some new thoughts he had which would create a different path for him going forward.

"Heather, I have a completely new concept to use with my most unique photos, including trying to buy back two special pieces of photo art I sold, and then combine those with *The Waterfall* grouping I now have."

Heather was not prepared for this approach and was a bit confused. Brian was no longer selling photos for income; they had money from the sale of his parents' home, the lawsuit settlement, and she was still getting money from the trust fund set up by her own grandfather. So, what was he going to do with the photos he had worked so hard to create?

"Brian, are you saying you feel they are too unique and important not to share in some other way?

"Exactly!" responded Brian. "I want to donate them using some type of permanent loan to the Museum of Modern Art in New York, where more people can see them. I would get more credit nationally for having created them."

Heather sat back, stunned. That thought certainly had never entered her mind. After a few moments of thought Heather smiled and told Brian, "You're doing it again. Just when I thought you had nothing new to offer to me or to others you are inventing something out of the box!"

Brian and Heather took some time to catch up on other items that were still on their to-do lists before he started the process of trying to track down the buyers of the two pieces of photo art and buy them back. Brian called Rudy in New York to discuss his plan and ask for his assistance in getting his photos back. Rudy was taken aback the same way Heather was at first.

"Brian, if you pull this off, you could make the cover of Time Magazine!"

Brian laughed and told Rudy, "That's a bit of a stretch Rudy, but how should I proceed to find and get his photos back?"

"I think I can be of some assistance, but I want something in return. Will you promise if we're successful getting these very unique and important photos back, and if you are interviewed by the media, would you, in some way, find a way to help promote my studio as a part of this story?"

"Of course I would! Let's meet to put something in writing that covers our deal."

"Brian, I know you well enough at this point to skip formal agreement. I will take your word instead."

When they were off the phone, Brian sent an email to Rudy authorizing him to reach out to the buyers of the photo art pieces and request that they accept a call from Brian if he contacted them.

The easiest person for Rudy to reach was Eileen Harrington. He explained that Brian wanted to contact her and received her permission on the first attempt Rudy made. Rudy passed along Eileen's contact information in Florida to Brian and continued to try to reach the buyer of *The Warehouse* grouping.

When Brian called Eileen, she warmly welcomed his call.

"Eileen, I was so sorry to learn about Daniel's passing. Please accept my sincerest condolences."

"Thank you, Brian. Daniel thought a great deal of you. So, Rudy called me and said to expect your call. How can I help you?"

"Do you still have *Man on a Bench*, Eileen?"

"Why, yes, Brian. I brought the *Man on a Bench* piece to Florida with me when I moved from the Hamptons. I have it, but it is still in a wooden moving crate in my condo, and I have not figured out what to do with it. Even though Daniel was in love with it, and I thought it was both clever and beautiful, I never unpacked it for two reasons. I don't have a wall large enough to display it, and it would bring back sad memories of Daniel because I knew how much he loved that piece of art."

Brian offered to pay Eileen ten percent more than Daniel had paid for the piece and pay the shipping cost to get it from her condo to Brian in Courtland. Eileen immediately agreed to that offer and only asked Brian to send an email with his offer. She would then release the art to any shipper Brian hired to get it to him. Brian had the email sent within an hour, informed Rudy that he had succeeded with Eileen, and asked how he was doing with the *Tired, Lonely Warehouse* photos.

Rudy then let Brian know he had been able to reach that buyer who was also willing to take a call from Brian. Brian made contact with the buyer of the *Tired, Lonely Warehouse* set and made the same offer to him as he had with Eileen Harrington. The buyer accepted Brian's offer of receiving ten percent more than he had paid, stipulating Brian would pay for shipping the piece back to him. This buyer asked why Brian wanted the warehouse photos back. When he learned Brian wanted them to be seen in one of the most famous museums in New York he had no issue with Brian's offer.

When Brian received both the *Man on the Bench* and the *Tired, Lonely Warehouse* photos he placed them against a wall in his office, stood back with his arms folded for some reflection and perhaps self-admiration. Heather had entered Brian's office and caught him in a great pose, grabbed her cell phone, and took a photo of her husband admiring his own work. For someone who had no experience taking professional photos and just using her phone, she had captured a great shot. Brian had not seen her take the photo, so Heather quietly walked back out of his office, wondering how to create something special with that photo.

Brian called Mike to bring him up to date.

"Mike, I have acquired both the *Man on a Bench* and *Old, Tired Warehouse* photos. Where are we in the process of getting them shown along with *The Waterfall* in the Museum of Modern Art in New York?"

"Brian, I will represent you at no fee and will start the process using the correct legal paperwork and follow up with the officials at the museum. Then I will get back to you."

"Thanks, Mike. I am tired and think I've earned some time "away." Perhaps I needed a getaway with Heather. I don't think I've been spending enough time with her while I was trying to piece this whole new art collection and museum idea together. I'll wait to hear back from you."

Brian brought Heather up to date about his call with Mike during dinner. Heather had been getting to know the Courland area, meeting neighbors and waiting for Brian to complete what she knew was one of the most important missions he had started since beginning to take photos professionally. When Brian mentioned he had to wait for Mike to get back to him, and thought he, Heather, and Flash should do something to celebrate together, Heather was on board immediately. But, where should they go, and what would they do?

"Why don't we each make a list of five places where we should go and what we would do on a getaway and tomorrow compare notes?"

"I think that's a great idea!"

They finished having dinner, Brian took Flash for a walk, and then Heather and Brian watched a movie while writing notes on a notepad they each had for getaway ideas to be discussed the next day.

At the end of that day, a more relaxed Heather and a much more relaxed and happier Brian headed for bed with thoughts of what may come next in their heads. Flash sensed something had changed with respect to Heather's mood, but what did he know? He was only a dog, right?

Chapter 36: Oh No, Not Again!

The next morning, after Brian took Flash for a walk, he and Heather sat down for breakfast to discuss where they each wanted to go for a getaway and vote on a winner. Heather was grinning and, in a childlike way, asked to go first.

Brian sat back, arms folded across his chest and told Heather to fire away.

"Okay, let's fly to Hawaii and stay there for a week, or return to Park City, Utah for another ski trip, or fly to somewhere in Florida and explore the state, including all the theme parks, or go to somewhere in Europe and then take a cruise after they get there, or return to where they had met in Central Park and have a picnic."

She looked up from her list at Brian, who had not moved or changed his position with his arms still folded across his chest. He hesitated to add a dramatic moment, then proceeded with his list.

"Let's go to a local gun range and I'll teach you how to handle firearms, and we will buy weapons for self- defense (he glanced up and saw the smile disappear from Heather's face), or fly to California and then drive to one of the major national parks where we can see the giant redwood trees together, or visit Vermont for the first time since neither of us has ever been there, or visit Chicago for the first time since neither of us has ever been there either, or return to where we met in Central Park and have a picnic."

Heather let out a scream, exclaiming, "You're kidding!"

Heather had considered listing her last choice first but was afraid Brian would immediately reject it. Brian started laughing because he was thinking the same thing. There was nothing more to discuss, only one place on both of their lists, and in each case, it was actually their first choice. That was all it took. Flash was startled when Heather screamed and then watched with interest when both Heather and Brian began laughing and acting silly. Flash relaxed and waited for a signal as to what was happening. Brian and Heather realized they had scared Flash, got down on the floor with him, and gave him a big hug. They each gave him a treat, telling him everything was fine, at which time Flash began wagging his tail. People who do not own pets may not always understand how close a relationship between pets and their humans can become to both the human owners and the dogs or cats they care for. Pets become a part of the family. In Flash's case, he was just that, but a lot more receptive to the feelings of his humans and had a keen understanding of their moods, even without direct communication.

Brian suggested that, since he had all the photo art back but had not yet heard from Mike, they should not wait to take their trip back to Central Park. The weather was moderate for January, and even though there was measurable snow on the ground, including in Central Park, there was no reason to put off their desire to get away for a day.

Heather called Amy to check in and to let her and Kevin know what had just been discussed, including how their lists matched.

"Amy, you aren't going to believe this. Brian and I each made lists for a getaway, and on each of our lists we selected one item that was the same, going back to where we met in Central Park and have a picnic!"

"That's hysterical. You and Brian have always been and still are on the same page, even if he has not yet brought up a proposed wedding date." Amy knew Heather had been patiently waiting for that.

The next morning, Heather prepared a picnic lunch for Brian and even made sure she had water and treats for Flash so they could get an early start from Courtland to Central Park. They did not want to rush and would be in traffic, but also wanted to have enough time together there to make their day worthwhile. On the way to their destination, Heather and Brian discussed some of the other things they each had been thinking about when spring came with respect to improving the landscaping around their home and some other items that they just had not talked about. Brian had been solely focused on his work, and Heather was still rearranging furniture in their home, so this was a unique opportunity to have an actual, uninterrupted conversation about things they had not discussed.

When they reached the parking lot close to where they had found the man who had been sitting on a bench completing a crossword puzzle they parked, took the picnic basket, and started a slow journey in the general direction where they had first met. Flash was busy sniffing the ground through the snow, seemingly remembering he had been there before. They found the now famous (to them) bench to sit and have lunch. Flash initially sat with them and enjoyed a snack while looking around, watching the squirrels and birds, appearing totally relaxed.

As Brian and Heather finished eating lunch and stood to head back to Brian's Jeep, Flash stopped short and sat back down. He was staring at something in the opposite direction from where Brian and Heather wanted to go. Brian looked at Heather and then back at Flash.

"Come on, boy, it's time to head back home."

Flash sat still and quiet. Then, slowly, Flash stood and started to walk away from Brian and Heather, toward a line of trees in the park where they had not gone that day. The bench where they had lunch was about fifty yards from that tree line. Both Brian and Heather instantly knew this was not Flash's normal behavior pattern and remained still, watching him slowly advance toward the trees. Suddenly, Flash turned his head back in the direction of Brian and barked.

Brian muttered under his breath, "Tell me this is not happening, again."

Flash waited and barked again. Brian called out to him again,

"Flash, come back, it's time to go home."

But Flash did not move. Brian, becoming uncharacteristically frustrated, yelled out to Flash, "You have to be kidding!"

Flash barked again and began moving forward, away from Brian. Heather turned to Brian, looking scared.

Brian, maybe you should get out Flash's leash and just go get him. When we have Flash, we should return to the Jeep and leave."

Brian rejected Heather's suggestion. "No, we need to remain where we are."

Then Brian started to slowly follow Flash. When they had reached the tree line, both Flash and Brian stopped. Flash sat down and looked up at Brian. Brian's face drained of color as he took his cell phone out of his pocket and called Heather, who was waiting for them to return.

In a calm, even voice, he said, "Heather, we need to call the NYPD. Flash has found a body."

This time, unlike in Utah, Brian could see a man lying face down in the snow, not moving, and there was blood both on the body and in the snow.

Brian had conflicting thoughts about whether to check for a pulse or stand still where he was. Once again, fresh footprints were in the snow and he did not want to disturb a crime scene if he did not have to if he believed the man in the snow may be dead.

Heather started crying. "No, YOU call the police while I wait where I am."

She did not want to add more footprints in the snow, and she did not want to see a dead body. Heather believed she would be of better service to the police when they came to the parking lot to see her first, so she could direct them to where Flash and Brian were now waiting for them. Brian agreed and dialed 911. He explained where he was and what he was seeing, asking for assistance. Within minutes, an NYPD police car pulled into the parking lot where Brian had parked the Jeep. The two officers who arrived at the parking lot saw Heather, who was waving, and headed in her direction to meet her.

When the officers, one male and one female, reached Heather, they identified themselves and asked what was wrong. Heather was trying to maintain her composure while she pointed in the direction of the tree line and told them her fiancée and their dog had found a body. All they had to do was follow their footprints, as they were less than an hour old. The male officer headed in Brian's direction while the female officer started asking Heather questions about why they were in the park and for her identification. While Heather was explaining why they were in the park, the male officer called the female officer and told her they had a dead body and to request a supervisor as well as detectives from robbery/homicide come to the scene.

When Heather overheard the request for more backup, she became emotional from the memories she still had from her experience in Park City and was shaking at this point. The officer with her permitted Heather to sit down on the bench, asking her to remain there while they all waited until the additional personnel could come to their location. About twenty minutes later one NYPD police supervisor followed by two NYPD detectives in plain clothes arrived.

The supervisor and one of the detectives, who identified himself as Jimmie Doyle, went to the scene where Brian, Flash, and the male NYPD officer were waiting while the second detective, who identified herself as Anita Sanchez, began to ask Heather the same questions she had just answered for the other officer who had stayed with her. She was now standing, becoming frustrated and scared. Heather knew they had done nothing wrong, but her experience in Park City was creating issues for her. She did not want to even mention that experience to explain her emotions, so she just tried to collect her thoughts, remain calm, and recount why she and Brian were in the park. She also stated, without knowing why she said it, that until Brian had returned, she did not want to answer any more questions.

Heather overheard Detective Doyle call Detective Sanchez and tell her they were also going to need someone from the medical examiner's office and a "bus" to come to the scene. In addition, he mentioned over his cell to Detective Sanchez, who was standing directly next to Heather, that the dead man had identification indicating he was not from New York but was from Salt Lake City, Utah.

When Heather heard that, she blurted out "NO!" falling onto the bench in tears, startling Detective Sanchez. Heather suddenly realized she and Brian needed to prepare to be in the custody of the NYPD the rest of the day, answering questions while trying not to say or do the wrong thing, which could more deeply involve them in something neither she nor Brian did. Her Park City experience had already influenced her emotions. That situation continued to flood her with bad memories, but she did not want her experience in Utah repeated now in New York.

Finally, Heather could see Brian and Flash walking back toward her with Detective Doyle. As they approached, Heather could see there was no color in Brian's face, and he was looking grim and not making direct eye contact with her. When Detective Doyle reached the park bench, he spoke to Brian and Heather.

"You both need to remain where you are." Doyle then asked his partner to walk with him a few feet away from where they could speak privately. Detective Sanchez then told Doyle about Heather's reaction to hearing the dead man was from Salt Lake City.

After the two detectives spoke for a few minutes longer, Doyle asked Brian and Heather to voluntarily come with him and his partner to the police precinct and continue to answer some questions. Heather remained silent, looking toward Brian for a signal, but before either she or Brian could respond, Doyle repeated his request to Heather.

"Ms. Parker, Mr. Miller already agreed on our way back to the bench. And of course, you guys can bring your dog. You can drive your own vehicle. Detective Sanchez and I will lead, and an officer in a NYPD car will be behind your vehicle. You will only be kept at the precinct long enough to help us obtain a bit more information to help, so we can fill out our paperwork."

Heather nodded and said she both understood and agreed to go to the police station. She then asked, "When we get to the police station, will we be questioned separately?"

The detective looked up from taking notes.

"That is a strange question. Why would you ask if you will be separated?"

Heather suddenly realized her memory of how they were treated in Park City caused her to ask that question. Brian remained silent while Heather said, "I have seen that on TV." Her answer seemed to satisfy the detective, and they all headed for their respective vehicles.

On the way to the police station, Brian was at first quiet and then turned to Heather.

"Are you okay?" She nodded in silence.

"I should not have asked about being separated, but that was due to our experience in Park City."

"Yeah, I knew the minute you asked the question that it would sound suspicious. Don't worry, it's all going to be okay."

When they reached the police station, the desk sergeant suggested that the dog stay with him and went to get a bowl of water for Flash. Brian kneeled down.

"Flash, Heather and I will be right back. Stay here boy."

At that point, Flash sat. Then, detectives Doyle and Sanchez each asked Brian and Heather to follow them into separate rooms that had a desk and some chairs so they could provide formal statements. Heather turned to the Detective Doyle.

"You lied to us about being questioned separately."

She immediately realized she had blurted that out in anger and then also realized it was probably a mistake. Brian then spoke up.

"Heather, just go with Detective Sanchez and cooperate. I'm going to do the same, and then they will get to go home."

Heather's mood had visibly changed and was noticed by both detectives. After Heather was seated at the table in the room where she had been led, Detective Sanchez leaned toward her and suggested that she was starting to think Heather and Brian may have something to hide. Heather did not know if this was a trick they typically use in similar cases or if she had triggered the detective into believing something was indeed wrong. Heather decided to try to get control of herself and the detective at the same time. Heather told the detective that she did not think she and Brian were being treated fairly as they were simply trying to spend some time in a park having lunch when Flash led Brian to a body.

Detective Sanchez sat back, folded her arms, and looked at Heather with a strange look on her face. This was not the normal behavior by someone who had just innocently found a body, and she was now thinking a different approach may be needed. She took out a business card along with a notebook and slid them both over to Heather.

"I need you to write down every detail pertaining to why you and Brian went to the park today while I go to talk to Detective Doyle, who is questioning Brian."

Heather realized she had triggered the detective and became angry with herself. While a uniformed officer remained in the room with her, she started a diary of why she and Brian had chosen to go to the park that day, being careful to leave nothing out, hoping Brian was doing the same thing.

She learned later from Brian that Detective Doyle basically asked Brian questions about his and Heather's day until Detective Sanchez opened the door and asked Doyle to step outside the room for a chat. Brian suspected something had either been discovered he knew nothing about, or Heather had said something that caused the change in procedure. He was right on both counts. When Detective Doyle came back into the room, he slid a legal pad with a pen over to Brian.

"I need you to write down every detail pertaining to why you and Heather went to the park today, and write down everything you know about someone named James Carter."

"Who is James Carter?"

"He's the man your dog and you found in the park. We identified him from his driver's license, which indicates he lives in Salt Lake City, Utah."

Detective Doyle never took his eyes off Brian when he provided that last bit of information. Brian was looking at the detective and suddenly realized something was definitely wrong. He and Heather were now persons of interest, not just innocent citizens who found a body.

Brian put the pad and pen down and pushed his chair back away from the table. He asked if he or Heather was under arrest or could go home. Detective Doyle responded with the fact that Brian and Heather were not under arrest but were material witnesses in a capital crime, which meant they could be held for questioning up to 48 hours if he or Detective Sanchez felt that the situation required it. He then suggested that Brian and Heather both cooperate, or they may be making matters worse for themselves if they did not.

Brian had no idea what Heather was saying in the other room and made a snap decision.

"Unless we are under arrest I want my cell phone back. It had been taken in the park. I now want to call my attorney based on your last comment. And I won't answer any more questions."

Detective Doyle stood up and just looked at Brian before abruptly turning and leaving the room. A few minutes later Detective Doyle returned and told Brian he could go and take Heather with him, but that was conditional on their signing a statement that they would not leave the New York area for at least 48 hours unless they called and received permission or were represented by legal counsel in that time frame. Brian signed the form, requested and received a copy of that document, and got up. Brian was then ushered out of the room where he had been talking to Detective Doyle and found Heather in the hallway sitting on a chair waiting for him.

"Heather, follow me to the front desk so we can get Flash. We're leaving." Heather remained silent as they left.

On the way home, Brian asked what she had told Detective Sanchez. Heather said she completed a diary of their day, but that was all. Brian then told her the dead man was from Salt Lake City, and he knew he was making things a bit more complicated for the detectives by requesting to speak to an attorney. Brian also said that when they got home, they were going to ask Mike to put them in touch with a criminal defense attorney who would begin representing them immediately. They would not volunteer to return or do anything further directly with the NYPD.

When Brian reached their home, it was late. Both he and Heather were tired, concerned, and angry. Brian reached Mike and told him what had happened in the park, and asked him to refer himself and Heather to a criminal defense attorney because he felt they had done nothing wrong. The fact that the dead man in the park was from Salt Lake City may have changed everything with regard to how they should now agree to cooperate with the NYPD. Mike agreed and said he would call back as soon as possible with the name of someone he could refer them to for criminal legal representation.

Heather and Brian were too tired to eat dinner, so they just sat in the family room, each with a beer, going over the details of the day. Brian was angry that a day they had set aside for themselves had been ruined when something neither of them had done wrong got in the way. Heather was just too exhausted to talk anymore and went to bed. Flash stayed with Brian, looking up at him and waiting for a signal. Brian looked down at Flash.

"Let's go for a walk, pal."

Flash immediately got up and headed for the door. Brian needed to clear his head and find a way to relax before calling it a day and joining Heather in an effort to get some sleep. The walk felt good, and Flash seemed okay, so after about thirty minutes, they both went back up the driveway. While Brian locked up and turned off the lights, Flash headed into Brian's and Heather's bedroom to his own bed and flopped down for the night.

Early the next morning, Brian received a call from Mike with a referral to Charles Hamilton, an experienced criminal defense attorney in New York City. Mike suggested Brian call Chuck's office as soon as possible.

"Chuck?" asked Brian. Mike responded

"I have actually known Charles a long time. I suggest you start with Mr. Hamilton and then ask him how he likes to be addressed by his clients."

Mike spoke to Brian about how he and Heather should proceed by getting representation quickly to show the NYPD they were serious and that many people in similar situations just use the phrase "I am calling my lawyer" as bluster. Brian agreed to call as soon as they were off the telephone. Mike also told Brian he had spoken to someone at the Museum of Modern Art, but still needed more time to determine if Brian's photos would be welcome there and to also learn more about the legal process. He said he would call Brian as soon as he had more answers. Brian thanked Mike again for helping with both situations and said his next call was to Charles Hamilton.

Brian was able to speak directly to Charles Hamilton on his first try. Charles suggested Brian call him Chuck and then asked for a brief summation of what had occurred the day before between himself, Heather, and the NYPD. After hearing Brian's side of the events, he suggested they come to his office for consultation as soon as possible, that day if possible as he was not scheduled in court. Brian agreed, scheduling for both Heather and him to meet with Chuck at 1 PM that afternoon. Brian then thanked Chuck for offering to see Heather and him so quickly.

When Brian was off the phone with Chuck he told Heather, who had just showered after sleeping late and was heading for the kitchen, that they had a meeting with an attorney.

"We are going to meet with Chuck Hamilton today. Mike had suggested this attorney, we have already spoken, and now we need to go into the city and be on time for our 1PM consultation."

Heather seemed relieved that they would have legal representation that quickly, had breakfast, and agreed to be ready to go when Brian suggested they leave.

The meeting between Brian, Heather, and Chuck Hamilton lasted about an hour. Chuck asked a series of rapid-fire questions while taking notes as he went. He quickly surmised the reaction by the two detectives was solely based upon Heather's reaction to learning the dead man was from Utah because they did not have time to put together the fact Brian and Heather had ever been to Salt Lake City, and neither Brian nor Heather had volunteered that information. Chuck suggested that, since Brian and Heather were referred by Mike, someone Chuck had known for several years, there was no need for Chuck to request his usual minimum financial retainer of ten thousand dollars yet. But, he did need Brian and Heather to each sign a formal Letter of Engagement and each pay him one hundred dollars so Chuck could legally represent Brian and Heather when speaking to the prosecutor, a woman named Sara Rubin, who worked out of the precinct where Brian and Heather were questioned by detectives Doyle and Sanchez.

Chuck apologized for the duplicity of two agreements and two retainers, but because Brian and Heather were only engaged and not married, he had to treat them as individual clients. Brian and Heather each signed a separate agreement, and each wrote a check to Chuck's firm as requested, stating they understood and thanked him for his representation. They knew they had done nothing wrong and wanted this matter to go away as quickly as possible, hopefully without having to return to the police station for additional questioning even if the police learned in the coming days that Brian and Heather had been to Salt Lake City. Brian, Heather, and Chuck shook hands, and Chuck agreed to follow up and then be in touch regarding the situation in the park.

On the drive back to Courtland, Brian still felt a bit uneasy and sensed Heather also had some concerns about having to return for more questioning. He suggested the following to Heather.

"First, why don't you go out to dinner tonight, somewhere that serves alcohol? And second, while at dinner, we should have a do-over with some new places for a getaway."

With that, Heather broke out laughing. Brian always had a way of knowing the right thing to say at the right time.

"I think that's a great idea, especially somewhere where I can get a drink. But I think we need to put off any further getaway conversations for now."

In her mind, it was not lost on Heather that she needed to sign her own Letter of Engagement and pay Chuck a retainer separately as she and Brian were still not married. While happy she had representation, the other matter was still stuck in the back of her mind as a question. Were they getting married anytime soon?

Chapter 37: Mixed News

Within two days, Brian received another call from Mike regarding what he had learned about showing his photos at the museum and a call from Chuck with an update about the Central Park episode.

"Brian, the museum is open to what you suggested, but they follow strict protocol regarding what art can be shown there. You would need to make a formal in-person presentation to a committee established for that purpose. Then senior management would need to receive a good review and recommendation from that committee before moving to the legal aspect of having something there on loan."

"Okay, can you help set up a meeting with the committee on my behalf?

"I'd be happy to do that. Be back in touch."

Chuck's call came on the same day as Mike's.

"Hi Brian, my conversation with Sara Rubin went very well. Sara interviewed both of the detectives regarding the suspicious death of the man you found in Central Park. She then got back to me and assured me no follow-up will be needed with you or Heather at this time. She did, however, reserve the right to bring you both back into the precinct for additional questioning if she felt it would be needed, but would call me first to set up a convenient time for all parties to meet. I pressed her harder, Brian, and then Sara repeated that there did not seem to be any direct connection between the dead man found in the park, you, or Heather, and apologized if you were left with the impression you were suspects or going to be charged with a crime."

After Brian had concluded both calls and could put his thoughts together, he called Heather, who was shopping for groceries.

"Hi, guess what? I have heard back from both Mike about the museum and Chuck about the NYPD. I can give you more details when you get back home, but the bottom line was Mike is still working with the museum on my behalf to get my photos shown, and Chuck's feeling is that there will be no follow-up regarding the Central Park episode."

Heather pulled over into a parking lot and broke down in tears. She had not said much since they got back from their meeting with Chuck but had been concerned about what she and Brian might still have to do if they were suspects, including going back into New York City to prove they had nothing to do with that man's death.

Brian heard Heather sobbing. "Maybe you should take a break so you can drive and then come back home." Heather agreed and ended the call.

Brian took Flash for a walk in the mild end of winter weather to think about the many things that had been on his own mind, including his photos, the museum, the Central Park episode, as they were calling it, and his life in general. He still felt somewhat unsettled about his own future going forward and wanted more time away from photography until he heard from the museum. He decided to end his walk with Flash and head home. When he got home, Brian went directly into his office, turned on some relaxing jazz, poured himself a drink, and jotted down some of his thoughts to help him clear his head.

When Heather arrived home with groceries, Brian came out of his office to help her put everything away in the kitchen. Heather then turned to Brian.

"Do you think we could just go into the family room and talk?"

Brian was not sure what that meant, as Heather seemed more serious than usual and agreed to her request. They each got comfortably seated, Brian with a freshened drink in his hand and Heather with a cold beer in hers. Then Heather began.

"Brian, I want to take a trip back to Boston to see my parents, alone."

Brian put down his drink

"Heather, is everything okay?"

Heather hesitated for a few moments before responding.

"No, Brian, it is not. I have been thinking about the many things ahead in my life, while you have been concentrating on yourself. I am not angry or upset but I need some "me time" and I miss my parents too. They are getting older, and I have been through a lot of changes in my life recently. While I think a "get-away" with you would be nice, at this point in our relationship I just want to go to my Boston home for a few days."

Brian was momentarily rocked back in his seat, wondering what she was not telling him. His mind started racing through their conversations about mutual goals, ambitions, the purchase and furnishing of the house, the car purchases, Brian's travels to get photos, and of course the Central Park thing. What was not on his radar was the fact that Heather had been waiting for Brian to bring up a proposed wedding date.

Brian stood up and offered Heather a hug.

"I fully support you taking a trip to Boston anytime you want to go."

Heather smiled, hugged Brian back, and left the room, leaving the beer on the coffee table. The next day, after calling her parents to let them know she was coming to Boston for a few days, Heather headed to Boston with more than luggage for a few days in the car. Brian was left with Flash in an empty house wondering what had just happened.

Chapter 38: History Is Made

The following week, Mike called Brian to give him an update.

"Hey, Brian, I just wanted you to know you now need to contact the museum and set up an appointment for a showing with the committee that needs to see your photos."

Brian thanked Mike and called as instructed, establishing an appointment for a presentation the following week. He realized that it seemed like a long time to wait, but that the committee was not just sitting around waiting for him to bring in the best photo art they had ever seen.

To remain busy while he waited until the following week, Brian decided he should probably create a storyboard or something visual to support his unusual set of photos he was preparing to present. He had to prepare to sell this idea to several people who did not know him and perhaps did not even understand how unusual the *Tired, Lonely Warehouse* idea was, how great the *Man on a Bench* photo was, or *The Waterfall* photos. This would keep him busy and his mind off the fact that he was alone in the house with Flash, and for some reason, Heather was in Boston with her parents.

When the following week came, it was time for Brian to make his presentation to the special review committee at the museum. He called Mike.

"Hey, Mike. I've got a favor to ask. Would you possibly be available to meet me at the museum for moral support?"

Brian had spoken to Heather only once since she had been gone, and while everything sounded okay, he was getting nervous about his now rocky relationship with Heather.

"Sure, Brian, I just checked my calendar, so I'd be happy to meet you there. Let's meet at the museum thirty minutes before your presentation. We don't want to be late, right?"

Brian arrived at the museum on time and found Mike waiting for him at the entrance, looking like the attorney he was, professional, in a suit, and smiling. Brian had gone casually dressed, looking like a professional photographer, at least in his mind. They entered the museum with Brian carrying all three pieces of art, as he was now referring to them, and went through security. They were then escorted to a conference room.

When they entered, Brian and Mike found a dozen or so men and women sitting at a long conference table with notepads in front of them, looking like they were ready for a professional presentation. Brian was greeted by the chairman of the committee and offered refreshments, including the typical assortment of pastries and coffee. He politely declined and asked how he should proceed while Mike took a seat away from the table and remained silent.

The chairman of the committee then spoke. "Brian, feel free to begin your presentation when you are ready. Do you need any audio or visual aids to assist you?"

"Thank you, no. But I do have just one request. Could the staff at the back of the room dim the lights a bit around the table and aim the spotlights at the front of the room a bit better? I am going to set up my art on the easels that are already in place." The staff immediately accommodated his request.

As Brian removed each piece of photo art from his leather portfolio carriers and carefully placed them on the easels, he told the story he had memorized which explained what made each piece so unique in the world of professional photography and why he believed they should be shared with the public rather than hidden in a buyer's home, hung on a wall where very few people would ever know they even existed. His presentation took approximately thirty minutes, during which time Brian spoke directly to the committee, carefully watching for facial or other reactions regarding his presentation. He felt he had the attention of everyone in the room and was seeing nods and smiles while some committee members even took notes. When he was finished with his presentation, he asked if anyone had any questions.

At first, there was complete silence that seemed like a lifetime to Brian. Then one of the committee members spoke.

"Brian, I feel I must commend you on your attention to detail and the quality of your work. Someone else would have ended up with snapshots, but you really have created art."

Brian felt himself exhale as he had been holding his breath. Then another committee member asked Brian where each of his ideas came from, and if he had been inspired by something he had seen in a magazine or in an ad somewhere.

"Thank you, those are great questions, and logical as well. Each piece was my own unique idea. I have never seen any other work like the photos I just presented. I want to assure the committee that what you are seeing is totally from my own original thinking, and I have even copyrighted each piece to make sure nobody would try to copy my work when they become public."

That seemed to satisfy several committee members who were now talking among themselves and comparing their thoughts even before Brian had left the room.

One more person had a question and raised her hand.

Brian smiled. "I see a hand up. Please, feel free to ask me anything."

Brian was expecting to hear something about his camera lenses or settings from someone familiar with photography. The person who raised her hand had something else on her mind.

"Brian, why did you come alone today? Specifically, why did you not bring both of your partners who helped you, as mentioned in your presentation? You mentioned Heather and Flash were a part of your effort in your quest to become one of the best and most unique photographers in the world."

Brian had not expected that question, and it took him a moment to collect his thoughts. When he regained his composure, he smiled again.

"Thank you for your question. You are correct that I had the full support and assistance of Heather Parker, but she had to be in Boston to be with her parents today, so she could not be here. And, as for bringing Flash into the museum, well, I thought that it might be inappropriate protocol. But I want to give credit to the art studio owner for his assistance and to the people who had purchased my art. They have allowed me to buy my art back so all the pieces could be shown publicly, or I would not be standing here showing it to this committee today."

That response received smiles and a round of applause, with the committee chairman going to the front of the room, shaking Brian's hand, and congratulating him on an excellent presentation worthy of the committee's consideration.

At that point, the lights that had been dimmed came back up, then one by one, each committee member who had been at the table approached Brian and shook hands with him, praising his work and thanking him for sharing his photos and the stories that came with each. He was then told by the chairman that he should wrap up his art, and he would be receiving something more official from the museum after the committee had an opportunity to meet privately and make their recommendation as to their findings.

After all the committee members left the room, Mike walked up to Brian and, while grinning, shook Brian's hand.

"Brian, all I can say to you is I think I just witnessed history being made. I have been told it is extremely difficult to get art approved for display in this museum, and not to expect any reaction or immediate indication of approval from the committee. That was clearly not the case today when your presentation was over."

Mike helped Brian pack his photos, and they were then escorted back to the entrance and out of the museum. As they walked down the steps and prepared to part company, Mike turned back to Brian again.

"Drive safely and keep your mind on getting home. I am certain your photos are going to be the next big thing exhibited in the museum, and you are going to receive national, if not international recognition for your work."

Mike headed back to his office, and Brian walked to his Jeep for his drive home, feeling euphoric and relieved. He was exhausted but feeling very pleased with how things had just gone and could not wait to call Heather to share the news.

Brian made an effort to drive home slowly and carefully as he knew he was distracted by all the thoughts that were now going through his head. He had not wanted to get too hopeful about the reception he would receive at the museum, but now he could see magazine articles and perhaps even being interviewed on one of the local television affiliates in New York when his photos made it into the museum. He also decided to wait until he was home before calling Heather, for two reasons. He needed to concentrate on getting home, and he wanted to be as relaxed as possible when he told her about what he had just experienced. He was also wondering how Heather would accept this great news, considering the fact that she seemed distant and upset when she left to go to Boston.

When Brian reached home, he was met by a little black and white border collie who had been anxiously waiting for his partner and best friend to return home. Without Heather at home, Flash had to wait to get the news from Brian about how his meeting went. Do dogs really understand human behavior that well? We may never know. What was true in this case was that Flash received the biggest hug ever and even a treat immediately after Brian came into the house. Brian finally felt settled enough to call Heather.

"Hi, how are things in Boston, and how are you doing?"

"Hi, Brian. Things are okay here. Anything I should know about?"

"Well, things are okay here, too."

Then Brian blurted out what had happened that morning at the museum, and Heather seemed to brighten up a bit. The call was short, and then Heather said she needed to go. Within minutes, Mike called.

"Brian, I hope you are sitting down. I just heard from the museum. In record time, your work has been approved, so you will need to go to the museum with me to sign some documents that will legally allow the museum to show your photos!"

When Mike and Brian ended their call, Brian reached into his mini-bar and pulled out an unopened bottle of rare scotch he had been saving for a special occasion. He poured himself a drink over ice, went into his office with Flash following close behind. He turned on some soft jazz and sat down to give himself a toast. While Brian fully realized he missed Heather terribly at this point, he was not going to wait for her to return to celebrate what had just occurred.

Flash received a treat from a bowl Brian kept near his recliner, then he sat back and tried to fully enjoy the moment. After finishing his drink, he looked down at Flash, who was looking up at Brian.

"Flash, you are the best friend anyone could ask for, and I love you."

Flash wagged his tail in appreciation and flopped down on Brian's feet while Brian dozed off.

Chapter 39: A Major Surprise

Through Mike, Brian had made the proper arrangements to drive back into New York City the following week, meet at Mike's office to read and sign the paperwork Mike had from the museum so Brian could then deliver his photos to be placed on display. All the work during Brian's journey to get his prized photos shown publicly in one of the best-known museums in the world was coming to fruition.

Heather was still in Boston after having been there a full week, so Brian decided to check in with her again to see how she was.

"Hey, stranger, how are things going in Beantown?"

"Hi, Brian, good to hear from you. I've made some preliminary decisions about what I want to do with my life when I return to Courtland. At the top of my list is going back to school to get an advanced degree in social work that would allow me to become a licensed practicing therapist. Then I want to find work in the Courland area. If you remember, this was part of my original plan before we became engaged. I feel I need to continue to move forward and create a full-time worthwhile position for myself while helping others in the manner I had intended to do, even while I was getting my four-year degree before moving to New York."

Brian listened and then responded, "That's great! I told you I would support whatever you wanted to do when you came back to

Courtland. Which brings me to my next question: how much longer do you think you need to be in Boston?" Heather hesitated, then said, "A little longer."

That same afternoon, Brian's doorbell rang while he was cleaning up some things around the house and thinking about his conversation with Heather. He was lost in thought and did not hear the bell ring. Flash barked once, walked to the front door, and sat. When Brian opened the door, a messenger was standing there.

The messenger looked at Brian and said, "I have a special delivery envelope for Brian Miller that requires a signature."

Without saying anything to the messenger, Brian signed the document, closed the door, and walked into his office to open the envelope. While seated at his desk, Brian opened the envelope and found a typewritten letter. What came next blew his mind.

The letter inside the envelope was addressed to Brian from a person who identified himself as Peter Jacobs who said he was living in New York City. The letter continued.

"Brian, this may come as a surprise, maybe even a shock to you, but I am your older brother. To find you, I had to do extensive research with the assistance of a private investigator. I am not sure if you knew what had happened to me or that our birth mother, Ellen Miller, had a brief affair during the time she was married to our father, Harold Miller, before you were even born.'

274

The letter continued.

"Through my research, I learned the family I have lived with since I was just an infant is my adoptive family, but I was never told I was adopted until about two years ago. At that same time, I learned my brother and sister, Harvey and Miriam Jacobs also had been adopted by my adoptive parents, Nathan and Sarah Jacobs, both of whom are now in various stages of ill health. When I confronted them about being adopted, they revealed to me that Harvey and Miriam had been adopted shortly after they were born as well. Harvey and Miriam both moved from the New York area several years ago and are not in communication with me anymore. It was only through my efforts to create a family tree with the assistance of the private investigator I hired that I was able to determine you, Brian, are my half-brother and actually living in the greater New York area."

Brian stopped reading the letter with his heart pounding out of his chest. He re-read the letter slowly in an effort to digest it completely and make sure he understood what this Peter Jacobs was saying. Is this really his older brother?! Is this the same older brother Brian asked about so many times when he was much younger, but had been unable to obtain any information about? Does this explain why there were no photographs of Peter in their family home? Does this explain why, when he repeatedly asked why there was no evidence in the home about Peter, he was told he did have an older brother who died as an infant, yet there were none of his personal items in their home at all?

Could it be that his parents decided not to keep Peter because of the affair his mother had, gave him up for adoption and then only considered raising Brian and Amy, who were actually their only biological children together? Brian read the letter a third time, this time wondering why Peter reached out to him even though Peter made it clear he was only trying to connect and sent the letter to allow Brian the opportunity to decide if he wanted to meet Peter Jacobs in person.

Brian broke out in a cold sweat, moved away from his desk leaving the letter there. He poured himself another drink of scotch, something he had been doing a lot more recently since Heather had gone to Boston, first to celebrate, now to steady his nerves. What was he to think? How could he verify whether any or all of this was true? What could this mean with regard to his financial situation, legally, if he had a living sibling in addition to Amy? And what would Amy think when she learned all of this? How would she take the news? Did Peter send her a letter too? Did she already know about all this? Or was Brian supposed to tell her, and if yes, how and when? Amy was expecting a child. Should this news wait until after she safely delivers her baby?

Flash had followed Brian to his recliner, watching him closely, sensing something was wrong. Brian noticed Flash just sitting and staring up at him and realized he had gone into shock. He reached down and comforted Flash.

"We need to go for a walk, buddy."

Flash immediately headed for the front door while wagging his tail. Of all the things Brian had experienced in his life, much of it now replaying in his head, this was the last thing he would have ever expected, and he had absolutely no idea how to handle it.

As soon as Brian and Flash returned from only a ten-minute walk, Brian called Mike.

"Hey, Mike. I need your help with something, and it's important."

Brian did not even give Mike his usual greeting, asking if Mike had time to talk or answer a question.

"What's up, Brian? You sound terrible. I'm going to grab a legal pad so I can take notes. Hold on." After a short delay, Mike returned. "OK, I'm ready. Try to remain calm and go slowly. What's wrong?"

Talking fast and not making much sense to Mike, Brian went through the letter he had just received by messenger, explaining he had just received the biggest jolt since the day he learned his parents had been hit by a truck and subsequently killed.

"Brian, take a breath and slow down. Are you sitting? You're not driving right now, are you? I know you, Brian. You've probably already had a drink. You can't drink and drive. You need water, and you need to stay hydrated so you can relax."

While Brian was on the phone with Mike, he began to relax and go over his thoughts with Mike more slowly.

"Mike, how can we verify what is in this letter before I even tell Heather, Amy, or anyone else?"

"We need to meet, Brian. I need to see the letter and most likely get some assistance with verification. We need to try to find a birth certificate for Peter, but also a death certificate. And we need to determine if there is a burial site for Peter and pursue the question if Peter died and is not in a cemetery or was cremated. All public records for Peter Jacobs need to be verified from the DMV and other public records. That is what we need to do. We need to cover a lot of ground before we try to arrive at any solid conclusion about what is in the letter you received. And one more thing. If, and I hope it doesn't come to this, if we can't verify whether Peter is alive or dead, I am going to suggest you consider getting a security system that includes cameras for your home in Courtland. Brian, I'm not suggesting this person may be a threat because if he wanted to confront you and do something bad to you, he wouldn't have written that letter and sent it to you."

Mike and Brian spent close to an hour brainstorming as neither had ever experienced a situation quite like this in their personal lives. At least Mike had resources to help Brian figure some things out before Mike suggested to Brian that they move forward to a face-to-face meeting with Peter. Brian agreed that it would not be a good idea until and unless they could verify that everything Peter said in his letter is true.

"Brian, I need to remind you about your meeting at the museum next week. You can't lose sight of that, and you need to give me some time to look into everything we've just discussed. I want to make some calls to get as much information as possible before we go to the museum. Scan and email the letter to me so I can have a copy to work from, and I can start looking for answers to all of the questions that need to be answered as soon as possible. You and I will figure out your next steps with Amy and with Heather."

After Brian and Mike ended their call, Brian disregarded Mike's advice and poured himself another drink. How in the world could his parents get rid of a child born to his mother, along with all evidence he had ever been a part of their family, and lie to both Brian and Amy without even blinking?

And why did they feel that was even necessary? To say the least, Brian's mind was running like a train, his heart rate was elevated, and he did not feel well. He had seen a call from Heather come in and let it go to voicemail. When he listened to the message, it was Heather advising Brian that she had decided she had been in Boston long enough and would be driving home the next day. Great! Not good timing. Brian had never lied to or held any important information back from Heather, how was he going to handle this? He only had one immediate thought. He needed another drink.

Chapter 40: More Surprises

Heather returned home from Boston the next day and found Brian sitting in his office with the lights dimmed, listening to jazz on a headset. He had not even heard Heather come into the house. Heather stood in the office doorway for a few minutes and decided to unpack and wait for Brian to come out of his office to greet her.

After an hour of waiting, Heather walked into Brian's office, moved directly in front of him into his line of sight and waved. Brian was startled, took off his headset, and stood to greet Heather with a hug.

"Hi! I apologize for not realizing you were home. I have been in my office thinking about a lot of things and trying to relax. How was your time in Boston with your parents?"

"Everything was fine, but I am tired from the trip. How about a nice, quiet dinner at home tonight?"

"Sounds great!"

Brian did not mention either his excitement about getting his photos into the museum or the letter from Peter. He had decided to wait for the "right time."

During dinner, Heather felt that something with Brian was "off." He seemed quiet and distant. He was friendly and in the room physically, but not really there.

"Is everything alright?' she asked quizzically.

"Uh, yeah, I just have a lot on my mind," came Brian's brief response, followed by him clearing the table and retreating into his office and back into his recliner, where he put his jazz on again, this time leaving off his headset.

Heather was tired from her drive back from Boston and was puzzled about Brian's somewhat "off" behavior but decided to head to bed early.

She leaned into Brian's office and, in a hushed tone, said, "I'm really tired from my trip and am heading to bed a bit early. I hope that's Okay."

"That's fine," Brian acknowledged with a wave. "I am looking forward to catching up with you tomorrow."

During the time Heather had known Brian, he had never seemed so distant, and she went to bed wondering if anything was wrong. And, if something was bothering Brian, why was he not sharing it with her?

When Heather awoke the next morning, Brian was already out of bed, had eaten some breakfast, and was on a walk with Flash. When he returned, he gave Heather a kiss on the cheek.

"Good morning, I need to run a few errands, Heather, but I will be back soon."

Before Heather could ask where he was going, Brian and Flash were already out of the house and in Brian's Jeep, going somewhere. Heather decided to call Amy to see how she was feeling and to ask if anything was going on with Brian that she should know about.

Amy answered and immediately told Heather 'I feel fat. I want to have this baby and get back to feeling normal."

Heather finally had the opportunity to ask Amy about Brian. "Amy, Brian seems "off." Do you know any reason why he would be that way, or if anything is wrong?"

"Nope, I haven't spoken to Brian for a couple of weeks. I wouldn't worry, though. Maybe you guys just need to sit down and talk. I need to lie down and get some rest. I am feeling really fatigued with the baby and all."

When Brian left the house, he was not sure where he was headed. He did not know whether or how to tell Heather about the letter from Peter and chose to avoid being in the house. He found himself in a park not far from the house where he could sit on a bench and let Flash run around a bit as this was a pet-friendly park. While Brian was sitting on a bench watching Flash run around Mike called with news.

"Hi, Brian. I have met with a private investigator I have known for several years to try and learn something about Peter Jacobs, and this is what I learned. Peter does indeed exist. We found birth records for a Peter Brooks, who was born exactly when you said he would have

282

been. Your mother's maiden name was Brooks. And there was no death certificate."

Brian just listened, and Mike continued. "Through social media and other public records, my investigator and I were able to locate a Peter Jacobs working as an architect with a New York City firm and living in an apartment in Brooklyn. There is no indication he is now or ever has been married, he has no record with the NYPD or New York state police, and he seems like just another man living a normal life."

Brian listened carefully, then asked, "Mike, did either you or your investigator search everything that was possible to search?"

Mike paused, then responded, "Brian, this man is real, he is your half-brother, and he is living in Brooklyn. I suggest you give some thought as to how and when to follow up if you intend to meet Peter in person. I also suggest you think about both Amy's and Heather's reactions to you when you tell them. Remember Brian, Peter reached out in the most professional and non-threatening way possible, only recently having learned he had been adopted, and he included his cell number so you could reach him if you wanted to follow up."

"Thanks, Mike. I really appreciate all of this information. I have a lot to think about."

Brian sat on the bench as Flash came over to him and jumped up onto the bench to sit next to Brian. After a few minutes, Brian turned to Flash and said, "Buddy, I know what I have to do."

Brian called Amy to ask how she was feeling. When Amy answered, she asked, "What is this, check-in on Amy day?' Then she laughed and explained that Heather had also called her about an hour earlier, asking the same question.

"Yeah, we decided to both call and bug you." Brian laughed and then continued, "Amy, are you up for some company?"

"Heck yeah, I'd love to see you guys!"

"No, I need to see you alone. Right now, I am not at home with Heather. I am in a park with Flash and just wanted to stop by to see you before heading home."

Amy invited him over, asking, "Is this a private meeting, or should Kevin be present?" Brian paused and responded with one word, "Private."

Within twenty minutes, Brian was inside Amy's home and sitting with her in their family room. Kevin was playing golf that day, which is why Amy asked if he should be there too. Brian did not waste any time and produced the letter he had received from Peter, handing it to Amy. She sat there stone-faced reading the letter, and then looked up at Brian with tears running down her cheeks.

"It's true!" she exclaimed, starting to cry. "I can't believe it!" she continued.

Brian sat there, taken aback. "You knew about this?" he asked.

Amy replied, "No, not everything. But I have known Peter did not die as an infant and never wanted to tell you because Mom had made me keep it a secret. I was very young when mom and I were having a mother-daughter talk, you know, about life issues. I was a teenager at the time, and she was trying to make a point about good behavior and not making some of the same mistakes she had made in her life. She told me that even Dad did not know she was telling me about Peter. She felt ashamed and embarrassed and wanted to make sure I made good decisions in my life, that's all. But she made me swear I would never tell anyone because of the legal issues involved in an adoption and because she would not want to have to relive the pain she suffered giving up her baby."

Brian sat back in stunned silence. He had mixed emotions about the fact that his own mother had kept this secret and that Amy had also still not said a word, even after the accident, now that their parents were gone. She knew they had a brother but had never once said a thing. He began to grow angry and felt he should leave before he said something he regretted.

Amy looked up at Brian when he stood, and she stood as well. "Brian, please don't be angry with me." She gave Brian a hug. "I love you, and I'm sorry I never told you anything about any of this."

Brian just stood there in silence, then stepped back.

"Amy, I understand your situation, but I need to go home and think. I need to figure out whether I want to meet Peter and also how or when to tell Heather. I am confused and a little upset. I think I should go home. But, again, I understand and I'm not angry with you."

Brian headed to Amy's front door as Flash followed, got into his Jeep, and drove directly home. When he entered the house, his first stop was the mini bar to get some scotch, and then he went into his office and sat down in his recliner to try to understand what had happened and get some perspective. Without him realizing it, Heather had seen Brian and Flash come in and then saw Brian heading into his office with a drink in his hand. She decided to head for the kitchen and bake something to avoid a conversation with Brian because she could see he was very upset.

Hours passed before Brian came out of his office to find Heather, who was still baking cookies in the kitchen.

"This looks like a bakery in here," he laughed. "What the hell are you doing? Cakes, cookies, and a pie?"

Both broke out laughing. Amy admitted seeing Brian come home and had decided to do something constructive until he chose to come out of his office and talk to her. She admitted feeling something was wrong but wanted to give him some space. Brian smiled.

"Let's go into the family room. I've got a lot to tell you."

Once seated, Brian slowly and methodically told Heather about his status with his photos, that they would be on permanent loan and displayed at The Museum of Modern Art in New York City, as he had hoped, and what he and Mike had to go through to make that happen.

Heather applauded and blurted, "That's great news! But now I want to know what made you so upset."

Brian pulled out the letter from Peter and handed it to Heather, then waited for her reaction while getting himself another drink and coming back to the family room.

"You have to be kidding!" exclaimed Heather. "Is all this true?"

"It is," replied Brian. "Mike and a private investigator verified it all. But there is more. Amy has known for years. I just came from her home. She admitted she had been keeping our mother's secret as she had promised."

Heather reached out to Brian and hugged him, starting to cry. She was starting to put her thoughts aside about her own uncertain future to be able to provide Brian with the support he now needed.

"What are you going to do?"

"I don't know yet" was Brian's only response. Then Brian took Heather's hand.

"Maybe we should go into the kitchen to find a sign by eating everything we can in the next fifteen minutes, starting with the cookies."

Heather broke out laughing. Brian was back!

Chapter 41: Figuring Things Out

In the days that followed, Brian and Heather did not leave the house. They spent time talking about their respective lives to that point, how they met, the path they had been on since meeting, dating, falling in love, moving in together, the trip to Utah, buying a home, and their brush with the NYPD. Then, Heather finally told Brian about her feelings about waiting for a good time to talk to Brian regarding a wedding date.

"Brian," Heather began, "I think it's been good talking about our past. But I've wanted to talk to you about our future. Since we are putting all our feelings on the table, and I do think we've waited too long to have a talk like this, there is one more thing I'd like to discuss."

"Really," Brian responded. "I agree. What else is on your mind?"

"Well, now that I am more up to date about what's been on your mind, to be honest, I've been waiting for an opportunity for us to discuss a...wedding date."

"Oh, wow! You're right. Getting engaged is one thing, but I've really been distracted for too long, and we have to put this on a list of things to figure out. Thank you for bringing this up."

Everything between Heather and Brian was now on the table for discussion, and this was the best and most open communication they ever had. The feelings they had for each other were not puppy love (no offence, Flash), but the real thing. They had both waited too long to tell each other how they were feeling about too many things, and realized it took Peter's letter showing up unexpectedly to bring them back together.

They needed to visit both Amy and Kevin to make sure the four of them formed a more solid bond going forward with no secrets among them. Finally, two more things needed to be addressed, meeting with Peter after figuring out how, when, and where. And, of course, setting a wedding date.

Heather and Brian followed up with Amy and Kevin the next day and invited them to a celebration dinner of things yet to come. A baby was getting closer to being born, so a baby shower was in order. Amy and Brian needed to contact Peter and set up a meeting. And, then invite him to join their family as an official member who would be welcome without reservation. Finally, Brian and Heather needed to plan their wedding in consultation with Amy and Kevin so as not to step on their big event on the way.

Following their conversation about all of the items that needed to be and were addressed, Brian, in particular, needed a little more time to look back at his life and wanted to do so in a quiet setting somewhere nearby with Flash. He had been on the journey of a lifetime and just wanted a few more minutes to make sure he was on the right road going forward.

Brian and Flash went to the park where Flash had played, and Brian had spoken to Mike. After only about an hour, Flash came over to Brian, jumped up on the bench and then licked Brian's face. Flash sat there just looking at Brian without moving. Brian looked down at Flash and gave him a hug.

"Everything is going to be okay, Flash. Don't get stressed! Ya know what?"

Flash's ears perked up as he listened to Brian.

"It's time to go home and begin the next chapter of our lives. That includes mine, yours, Heather's, Amy's, and Kevin's too. We all have to move forward."

Brian got up from the bench and started walking back toward his Jeep. Flash followed, wagging his tail. Those few minutes in the park did help Brian think more clearly.

When Brian entered the house, he found Heather quietly sitting in their family room. She had also been reflecting on her personal journey, much as Brian had just done in the park. She looked up with anticipation, knowing Brian had been somewhere nearby, making decisions for them, or at least for himself, and she wanted him to start their next conversation.

Brian sat down next to Heather and began.

"Have I ever told you the date my parents were married?"

"No," Heather responded.

"Well," Brian continued, "the actual date may not even matter, but what do you think about a wedding in the fall, when the trees are in their full splendor, it is cool and crisp outside, but there may be a fireplace nearby if we need to warm up?"

Heather's heartbeat started to increase. Being engaged is one thing, but setting a date to get married is another.

"Can you be a bit more specific?" Heather asked.

"I can see, in my mind, a small rustic combination wedding venue that is also a bed and breakfast, maybe not far from Courtland, in a beautiful, wooded area as a bonus."

Brian continued. "I can see an old-fashioned bed and breakfast that is operated by a lovely older couple who perform weddings. Maybe the husband is a retired judge but still licensed by the state to marry couples. Maybe at one point they added a wedding venue on the same land adjacent to the bed and breakfast. My vision is to get married in a family-owned and operated inn that provides a great atmosphere, privacy, and memorable experience for couples who want to get married in this small but warmly furnished venue, which is decorated at all times for couples who want a more intimate setting, but is large enough for perhaps a dozen or so guests. Then, following the ceremony, the newly married couple would have the perfect way to start their married lives together and simply be able to walk to a beautiful, intimate inn without going more than a couple of hundred feet away to reach the perfect cabin at this same location in the bed and breakfast portion of this wonderful, romantic, magical place. This is what I am now visualizing. What do you think?"

While Brian was speaking, Heather sat still, her eyes filling with tears.

"You mean the most beautiful place on earth is just a few miles away, and it is just waiting for us to make a reservation and send out the invitations?" Heather asked.

Brian smiled and said, "As you wish."

"Do you have a date in mind, kind Sir?" asked Heather.

"I do," responded Brian. I checked my calendar, and October 20th, jumped right out at me. What do you think?"

Heather sat there for a moment, looking like she was pondering whether to buy a castle or a corporate jet, and then replied.

"Well, kind Sir, I have followed your lead since the day we met, so I am not going to stop now. That sounds perfect!"

With that, Brian and Heather both stood and embraced while Flash jumped down from where he had been sitting on a chair, barked, and joined them in a group hug. Do pets, specifically a black and white border collie named Flash, really understand everything going on around them? Do we need to ask?

Chapter 42: Following Up

Brian and Heather called Amy and Kevin the next morning with two items of importance. First, Heather and Brian had set October 20th as their wedding day, and they wanted Amy and Kevin to be the first to know. The news was met with excitement and messages of congratulations from both Amy and Kevin. Heather suggested Amy and Kevin begin an invitation list of guests they would want to invite, keeping in mind that family had to come first, there would be limited space, and this wedding would be planned to keep it as intimate as possible.

After discussing the wedding plans now set for October, Brian brought up the subject of Peter and asked if Amy or Kevin had any suggestions about how or even if they thought Brian and Amy should follow up on Peter's letter. Kevin spoke first, something he rarely did.

"In my opinion, as a kind of an outsider in this situation, you, Brian, should be the one to call Peter and suggest that you and Amy meet Peter for coffee or lunch somewhere in New York where Peter would be comfortable. Hopefully, you guys can think of a place that is quiet and a bit private, but make it easy for everyone to break the ice and actually have a real conversation so you all can get to really know each other. If I was in Peter's position, I would want to feel welcomed into your family again, as it exists today. I guess he would welcome such an invitation. You guys have a big time gap to close."

Amy spoke next. "I want to remind you guys that's why I married Kevin, and I agree with what he just suggested, the right thing to do, and the best way to initiate contact while hoping to close a gap that has existed far too long. What happened to Peter is not his fault, and I don't suspect any nefarious intent with respect to Peter reaching out to you, Brian."

Heather went next. "I also agree completely with both Amy and Kevin. And Brian, I think you should make the call to Peter and learn if Peter is also in agreement with this kind of meeting."

Brian hesitated for a moment. "Well, the vote is 4-0. I agree with what everyone else has said and I will let everyone know more after I am able to successfully reach Peter and suggest that Peter, Amy, and I have lunch in the city – soon.

Following the call Brian sat down to gather his thoughts about how to introduce himself to Peter, keeping his tone in mind. He created speaking points to use on the phone call and explained how he and Amy would like to meet with Peter. Brian was both happy to have found a missing brother and nervous about meeting him for the first time.

Heather could see the wheels turning in Brian's head as he sat thinking about his next steps. Instinctively, Heather put her arm around Brian.

"Brian, you don't need to worry about the call or the meeting. Peter is not something you need to photograph in a perfect situation, nor would Peter expect you and Amy to just show up and act like you all have known each other for several years. This may be a bit awkward for you now, but if you, Amy, and Peter want to become closer and be a family unit as you all should have been from the beginning, the three of you will find a way to make it happen. And remember, Brian, both you and I supported Kevin and Amy in spirit and in love when we all met for the first time. We let them know that, and it has all worked out."

Brian smiled, stood up, and hugged Heather.

"You have always been my rock and my support. I need to go into my office now to gather my thoughts and then call Peter."

Heather called out to Flash. "Hey bud, this may be a good time for a walk."

As Heather turned toward the door, Flash remained seated and did not move, closely watching Brian, who was not aware Flash was looking at him until he stood up to go to his office. Brian turned to Heather, who was watching both Brian and Flash, and then looked at Flash.

"Go ahead, Flash, I'm fine. Go for a walk with Heather."

Flash quickly got up and headed for the front door. Brian shook his head, wondering what Flash really understood, and then went into his office, closed the door and picked up his cell phone to call Peter. When Brian heard the front door close as Heather and Flash left, he nervously dialed the phone number in the letter he was holding in his hand.

A man with a deep voice answered the call from Brian, "This is Peter."

Brian froze for a moment and responded, "And this is Brian."

Thus, the ice was broken. Peter hesitated for a moment and then spoke first.

"Brian, I was not sure if you would call."

"Peter, how could I not? Of course, I was taken completely off guard when I received your letter. I grew up believing that I had an older brother, but he died before I was even born. And to be honest, I actually did some research with the assistance of an attorney and a private detective to make sure you were real, and actually my brother. I'm just being honest with you right now. But I now realize you exist, and that we need to, or should, meet. I have a strong need to know you and then see if we can actually become a family, something that should have occurred a long time ago."

That started a business-like, brief conversation about the need to get together in the city at a quiet place for coffee or lunch, and that the meeting would only include Peter, Brian, and Amy. Peter and Brian checked their respective calendars and agreed to meet at a coffee shop familiar to them both the following week, on Wednesday at noon. The call lasted less than five minutes, and it was obvious neither Peter nor Brian really knew what to say to each other during this first call. It certainly felt awkward to Brian, and he was sure Peter felt the same way.

Following the call, Brian immediately called Amy.

"Hi, how ya feeling? Are you planning to deliver anytime soon?"

"Ha! I will deliver when I am good and ready. What is the real reason you're calling?"

"Amy, I just spoke to Peter. I am really calling to pass along that Peter and I agreed to meet in person next Wednesday at Noon at that cute little coffee shop called Mickey's in lower Manhattan. I told Peter you'd want to be there too."

"Wow! You did it, you really did it! I have nothing scheduled for next week so I will put the meeting on my calendar. But I'm going to tell you now, I would prefer to drive myself to and from the restaurant because I don't want you to have to provide transportation for me."

"No way, sister. I'll pick you up at 11 AM that morning. That is a long way for you to drive to and then back. I know you're only pregnant, but I won't take no for an answer."

When Amy began to protest, Brian interrupted her and said he wanted the support, at which time Amy laughed and agreed to let Brian pick her up and drive them to and from their meeting with their newly found, previously lost brother.

Brian dropped into his recliner and began thinking about all the years that had passed and the missed opportunities to know Peter because of the actions of his parents. He could not be angry with Peter and had to find a way to convey that. At the same time, he grew emotional and sad but then heard the front door open as Heather had just returned.

"Hey there, I'm in my office. I spoke to Peter and to Amy too."

Flash came running into Brian's office and took a flying leap into his lap, licking his face as if he could feel Brian's raw emotions from just making that phone call.

Heather walked into Brian's office and saw him crying and hugging Flash. She quietly turned and walked into the kitchen to get a cup of coffee and to give Brian some needed space. Words were not needed to explain what that first call meant to Brian. And, Heather felt it was better to allow him time to pull himself together before asking Brian what he wanted to do for dinner that night. It is not necessary to have a piece of paper that says two people are married if they are already on the same frequency. Heather and Brian had that connection, and they were both wise enough to recognize it.

Chapter 43: A Special Day to Remember

The day prior to the meeting, Brian called Amy.

"Hey Amy, this is just a reminder that I'll be picking you up bright and early tomorrow so we can get to the coffee shop on time."

"Oh, is that tomorrow?" Amy asked sarcastically. "Ya know, I'm still fine to drive myself, big brother. I wish men would stop treating pregnant women as if they were sick."

"No," replied Brian, "Not sick, just fragile, and carrying very important cargo."

They both laughed at the fragile cargo part of Brian's argument. Brian and Amy went back and forth for about five minutes until Amy gave in.

"Okay, you can be the MAN. See you in the morning."

Early the next morning, Brian called Amy again. "Hi, just your favorite pest checking in a bit early. How are you feeling?"

Amy was becoming a bit annoyed. "Have you considered setting up surveillance cameras and connecting directly into the baby's heartbeat so you can hear it?"

"I'm feeling some stress about the meeting and wanted to make sure you are still feeling OK. Oh, and I will be leaving soon to pick you up, which I know is earlier than we agreed yesterday, but I don't want to rush to be on time if there's traffic."

Amy responded again, "When you get here, I will be ready, with bells on!"

When Brian was on the way to pick up Amy, he was not entirely sure how to start their meeting. After he picked up Amy, Brian turned to Amy.

"I have some concerns about what to say and what to avoid. I want Peter to feel as comfortable as possible."

Amy suddenly felt a sharp pain in her abdomen and winced, "Oh! That was a sharp one."

Brian was concerned and asked, "Hey, are you okay?"

"Brian, relax. I am not due for another few weeks. Some pain is normal, just drive!"

When Brian and Amy arrived at the coffee shop, they found Peter already sitting at a table toward the back of the room. Peter determined it was Brian and Amy who had just come in and waved for them to walk back to where he had been sitting.

Peter then stood up to greet them, shaking hands with Brian and giving Amy a hug.

"Hey, guys, you're right on time! This is exciting!"

"Peter," Brian responded. "You have no idea how happy Amy and I are to have this meeting." Amy nodded, "I agree with Brian, we're totally excited to meet you."

A server came to the table and asked what they could serve Brian, Peter, and Amy.

Brian started, "Coffee for me, please." Peter spoke next, "I'll have coffee too." Amy spoke last, "I'll just have a glass of water and some crackers if you have some, please."

When the server left to get what everyone ordered, Brian continued speaking to Peter.

"I want to thank you again for reaching out and tell you one more time, Amy and I've been anxiously waiting to meet you from the day I received your letter."

"Thanks, Brian. And Amy, I know this situation can be stressful for you right now, but I am truly excited for you. I, of all people, know how important family can be."

Peter asked if he could explain a bit more about what happened to him when he was given up by their mother and subsequently adopted by the Jacobs family.

"I was too young to have any memories or know about my connection to the Miller family, but the Jacobs family has shown me nothing but love, and from my earliest memories to the present, that has not changed. My search for my birth parents and possible siblings was out of pure curiosity, and I was thrilled not only to find you both but even more thrilled you wanted to meet me in person."

All was going well until Amy suddenly screamed, slamming her open hand on the table, yelling, "Damn it!"

This startled Brian and Peter, as well as other customers in the shop and the servers. Everything and everyone suddenly stopped, and Amy became the focus of attention. Amy was starting to cry, so Brian leaned over toward her and whispered, "Is everything alright, Amy?"

"Hell no," Amy shot back, "My water just broke!"

Brian put his arm around Amy, "Try and stay calm, I'm here. Everything's going to be alright."

As Brian started calling 911 on his cell phone he continued speaking to Amy. "You need to try to stay calm. I know the city well, and there is a hospital just a few blocks away."

Amy, still crying, responded, "No, Brian, I am not fine. I am in New York City, and I am supposed to deliver my baby in Courtland!"

Peter tried to comfort Amy as well when suddenly Brian jumped up and headed for the door. He went to his Jeep and came back with a camera.

"What the hell are you going to do with that?" Amy shouted at

Brian.

Peter, attempting levity, leaned closer to Amy and told her he had read all about Brian's fame with his famous photos, including the group ones. He then asked her, "You aren't having twins, are you? Or triplets?"

Amy looked at Peter like he had just landed from Mars and was reaching for something to throw at him when two strong young men approached the table.

"Hi, I'm Jake, and this is Alex. We're both firemen at one of the NYFD's most famous station houses located not far away. We are also both EMTs and may be able to help. And I think I can already hear a siren."

Everyone stopped. Amy looked at Jake and responded, "There is no siren, Jake. This is a nightmare!"

Alex whispered something to Jake, then leaned closer to Amy and quietly said, "I know you don't know me, but I have personally delivered three babies in the past year, and if you can relax, I am sure I can assist you before things get any more tense for you, which would not be good for either you or your baby who obviously has made other plans for you to today than wait so you can deliver in Courtland as you had planned."

Alex had an immediate calming effect on Amy.

"What should I do if you need to deliver my baby?"

Brian and Peter were standing nearby, listening in total disbelief while Alex was calming Amy down like magic. Brian also realized that perhaps bringing a camera into the coffee shop was not a great idea.

Alex turned to the owner of the coffee shop and then to the other customers.

"I need everyone to please pay for their meals and leave the shop so Amy can have a little privacy."

The owner spoke up next, "I will check everyone out, please, let's do what we all can to help."

All of the customers in the shop went to the counter, paid for their meals, and quietly left the shop. Then the owner asked Alex, "What can I do to help?"

"Bring me a fresh, clean tablecloth, and some towels."

As he was rolling up his sleeves, Alex continued,

"Where can I wash up with a lot of soap and hot water?"

Amy began to stand while Jake held her steady and quietly said, "Amy, trust Alex. He knows what he is doing."

Jake then cleared the table, removing everything as the owner brought a freshly laundered tablecloth to cover it. Jake spread it out, pulled up a chair, and told Amy, "Here, take one step up on this chair, and hold on to me. Good. Now pull yourself up to a sitting position on the table."

Alex returned after carefully scrubbing his hands and arms.

"Peter and Brian, I need you both to move back so Amy can get more air and enjoy a bit of privacy."

Jake continued to talk to Amy, "I need you to lie back on the table and raise your knees."

Amy complied to Brian's astonishment as she had just gone from manic to calm in a matter of minutes, all because these two guys just happened to be in the right place at the right time. Because they were calm, she complied with their requests.

Alex called the 911 supervisor and asked how far away an ambulance was and got bad news. There had been a bad accident on one of the major highways not far away and all available EMTs were enroute to that incident. The supervisor suggested Jake, Alex, and Amy may be on their own if indeed the baby was "on the way."

Brian was close enough to overhear the conversation between Alex and the 911 supervisor, so he leaned down and whispered into Amy's ear, "Amy, you may have to give up some privacy and some dignity, but you need to trust these two guys."

Amy nodded. Alex was able to hear what Brian told Amy, smiled, and winked. He assured Brian in a whisper that he really needed to examine Amy to determine if this was a true emergency, and he needed permission to do so. Amy overheard Alex and told him to do what he had to do as she started to slip her jeans off while lying on her back on the table.

Jake asked the staff to return to the kitchen and stand by if needed, which they all did immediately. Alex and Jake both held Amy's hands and said they just needed to know if she could safely wait for help or if her baby was going to turn the day into "an event never to be forgotten in her life."

Amy had relaxed and stopped crying. She looked at both Jake and Alex, telling them, "Guys, I get what's happening. I fully understand the situation and appreciate the fact that you're both here. And, you have my full permission to examine me."

Alex checked the progress Amy's baby had made since Amy's water broke, then looked up and said, "Amy, nature is what it is, and so is medical science. You are about to give birth right here in the Big Apple."

Suddenly, Brian realized he needed to call Kevin and let him know what was happening. In all the excitement, he was privately embarrassed that he had not already done that.

Brian called Heather first to let her know what was happening. When Heather answered her cell, Brian blurted out, "You're not going to believe what's happening. Our meeting with Peter was going well, then Amy's water broke!"

"What? Are you kidding me?"

"No, I'm not. But, we got lucky. There are two EMTs here in the coffee shop from a nearby fire station. Amy is going to have to deliver here, and now. The baby's not going to wait to be delivered back in Courland. I need you to stand by in case I can't reach Keven. He's my next call."

Heather agreed, took a deep breath, and said, "Good luck to all of you. I'll stay near my cell phone."

Brian's next call was to Kevin, who was available to take Brian's call. "Kevin, I need you to stay calm. I am calling you from the coffee shop in the city where Amy and I were meeting with Peter. But Amy's water broke. Luckily for us, there are two EMTs here from a nearby fire station because the baby is not going to wait to be delivered as planned back in Courtland."

After a long pause, Kevin finally spoke. "Brian, I'm speechless. I need your opinion: Should I grab a cab and get to the coffee shop? Is Amy going to be Okay? This was not supposed to happen!"

Brian hesitated and then responded, "Kevin, if it was Heather, I would be on the way. But when you get here, you will need to remain calm so you can assist Amy and not add to the stress she is already experiencing."

Kevin agreed and got the address from Brian. "I'm on the way!"

Brian called Heather back to tell her Kevin was on the way to the coffee shop, and he would get back to her as things progressed. Heather said she would remain at home and would be ready to go to New York if needed. Brian decided to update Amy, Alex, Jake, and Peter about his call with Kevin.

He approached them all to bring them up to date, starting with Amy. But everyone else, including Peter, Alex, and Jake, could hear his conversation. Brian moved to the table where Amy was taking deep breaths and trying to remain calm as instructed by Alex and Jake.

He leaned over so he could hold her hand and then whispered, "Amy, Kevin is on the way in an effort to get here before the baby's born."

Amy smiled. "Thank you, Brian. Do you think Kevin can still get here before the baby comes?"

Brian shrugged his shoulders. "Amy, that's a good question, but it would be up to baby Brady at this point. I think you need to try to relax, stay calm, and follow the directions you are getting from Alex and Jake, and let nature take its course. From what I have observed so far, you are in good hands. I will let you know when Kevin arrives."

Amy smiled back again and then grimaced from a contraction. Brian realized he needed to get out of the way and let Alex and Jake take over. At this point, everyone in the coffee shop was a spectator, and whatever was meant to happen next would be impossible to predict. Brian kissed Amy on the cheek and said he would be nearby but needed to get out of the way.

Jake and Alex huddled with Brian and the coffee shop owner to explain what else they were going to need in order to proceed to help make this as safe a delivery as possible under the circumstances. They had to act as a team and help Amy remain calm. With no help on the way, Jake and Alex proceeded to assist Amy in doing what she had to do next, and that was to safely bring her baby into the world.

It took about an hour from the time that Amy's water broke, but then came the miracle fairy tale ending, a beautiful baby girl with blond hair and blue eyes who began to cry on cue as Alex placed her on Amy's chest so Amy could bond with her immediately.

Tears of joy streamed down Amy's face. And the staff, while still keeping their distance in the kitchen doorway, began applauding the firemen who had just made history in their little coffee shop.

The owner took Brian and Peter aside and asked if he could do anything for them, as they had been relegated to the sidelines for the big event. They both just shook their heads while smiling at Amy and keeping some distance.

Finally, an ambulance arrived. Two EMTs entered the coffee shop, met the shop owner, Alex, Jake, Peter, Brian, then finally Amy and her newborn baby girl. After a brief exam, they loaded Amy and her baby into the ambulance and took her to the hospital.

Brian and Peter thanked Alex and Jake, as well as the owner and his staff, for all the support they had provided.

Brian turned to Alex and Jake. "I don't know what we would've done if you guys hadn't been here. On behalf of Amy, her husband Kevin, and their baby girl, thank you, thank you, thank you, thank you, thank you, thank you!

Alex responded, "Jake and I actually see these situations more often than most people would believe. We are both just thankful we were here and able to assist. We want to wish you and your family the best, but I think we had better get back to the fire station."

When Jake and Alex left, Brian thanked the owner again, then turned to Peter. "Well, big brother, welcome to the family. Let's go to the hospital to check up on Amy and see Kevin. I just called him and sent him there instead of trying to get here now."

Peter agreed, and they left for the hospital, which was close by.

What an eventual first meeting for Peter, Brian, and Amy. It truly would be a date to remember.

Chapter 44: A Path Less Taken

A few days after Amy gave birth both Brian and Heather were spending time separately, thinking about what had happened and how lucky Amy was to have Alex and Jake in the right place at the right time. Amy and Kevin learned an important lesson. Sometimes the perfect plan can get changed at the last minute, but in the end, good health and total happiness are the two most important elements for any special occasion.

Brian and Heather were both home two days after Amy gave birth, each working on separate personal projects that needed attention. Heather was rearranging dishes, glasses, and silverware in the kitchen, and Brian was working in his office, filing away items that had been on his desk too long. He was reorganizing how he filed photos taken from the time he had begun working as a professional photographer.

Suddenly, Heather came into Brian's office and asked Brian if she could have a few minutes of his time.

"Brian, can I interrupt you to talk about something"?

"Sure, what's up"?

"I've been thinking about how fast life can change, like in a heartbeat, and especially how things changed at the last minute for Amy and Kevin. And, more specifically, the plan we discussed about how, when, and where to get married."

Brian stopped what he was doing and moved from his desk to the couch in his office. He suggested Heather sit down next to him. This sounded serious. Brian then turned toward Heather.

"Is something wrong? Are you having second thoughts?"

Heather burst out laughing, "Yeah, Brian, after waiting all this time for my big day, I don't want to get married anymore. Ha! You're right about second thoughts, but I'm just not sure I want to go through with our original plan."

Brian responded, "Okay then, what do you want to change? What would make you really happy?"

Heather paused and then continued.

"I'm almost afraid to admit what I'm thinking because I don't want to disappoint anyone in either of our families. But do you remember how you described our wedding? You suggested our marriage should include a small rustic combination wedding venue that is also a bed and breakfast, maybe not far from Courtland, in a beautiful, wooded area as a bonus."

"Yeah, I remember saying that."

"Well, maybe that's not what I really want. Maybe I just want to be married to Brian Miller and have a much smaller wedding, more private, with just us and a witness. I don't want to wait until the date you suggested. Amy's situation at the coffee shop started me thinking about making plans and then how they can get changed, but still focus on what's really important. Brian, if it wouldn't upset the entire family, I want to elope. I don't need a venue, or flowers, or music, or a ton of people at my wedding; I only need you."

"Wow!" was the first thing out of Brian's mouth. "I didn't see that coming. Are you sure about this?"

"Yes, life is short, things change, I want to be married to you, and I don't want to wait any longer to make it legal. Can you go along with this? Can we change our plans?"

Brian leaned over toward Heather and put his arm around her. Then he responded.

"Heather, we can do anything you want. All we need is to apply for a marriage license, wait 24 hours, find someone to perform the official ceremony, and we actually only need one witness. That's the law. The rest is up to us."

"Do you think people will be upset? I'm worried about my parents, Amy, and Kevin, too."

"Heather, let's do what YOU want to do, not what others want us to do. I met a very nice clergyman named Richard on the day my parents were killed. He was at the hospital. He was available at one of the worst times of my life to comfort Amy and me, and I will never forget how it helped. That was a sad moment. This is just the opposite. That man has a tough job, helping people grieve. How do you think he would react if he had the opportunity to officiate at our wedding, at a happy occasion, and see me again, but in a totally different situation?"

"Brian, you never fail to amaze me. You aren't upset; you roll with change. You've been through a lot in your life. And you want to include a person from your past who helped you cope and reward him with an opportunity to see you happy. I'd prefer to get married by Richard at that venue you suggested rather than a judge at the courthouse. And, if we do this, we only need one witness. Who would that be?"

Brian sat back, crossed his arms, and looked back at Heather.

"How'd you feel if we asked Peter to be there. I'd like to close that circle and give us a chance to make him a part of our family."

"Oh, my God! What a great idea! This is why I love you so much, another thought out of the box I'd have never considered, and I love it!"

Brian stood up, held out his hand, and helped Heather to her feet. He put his arms around her.

"Then we have a new plan. I will call Richard and Peter and see what we can figure out in terms of a date. We will still get married at the same place we had planned, but it will just be you, me, Richard, and Peter, right? And, you don't want to wait, is that right? We're going to just do this, and tell everyone after the ceremony that we eloped, right?"

"Yes! That's exactly what I now want. We'll take a few days to spend together after the wedding, and then I'll call everyone and explain what we did and hope for the best."

Brian looked back at Heather and responded, "As you wish."

Brian was able to reach Richard and Peter that same day and told them about their new plan. Both Richard and Peter were delighted to hear from Brian and agreed to play their respective roles in it. Heather and Brian drove to the courthouse and formally applied for a marriage license the next day, and Brian then called the bed and breakfast venue to reserve the day and time to get married there the following week.

Brian also made a reservation for a cabin at this same location in the bed and breakfast portion of this wonderful, romantic, magical place that was a part of the original plan, so Heather and Brian could just be alone, with Flash of course, for a few days. Then Heather and Brian made a trip to see Simon Stein the jeweler and purchased wedding rings.

The following week Brian and Heather executed their plan with Richard, Peter, and Flash present. Flash wore a red bowtie collar for the special occasion and was "Best Dog", carrying a small red box that was attached to his collar that held the wedding rings for Heather and Brian.

This is how Brian and Heather "tied the knot" and started their married life together. They took a different path, but in the end, they had each other.

"To have and to hold from this day forward, for better for worse, for richer, for poorer, in sickness and in health, to love and to cherish, till death us do part."

Chapter 45: What's Next?

When Kevin was headed to the coffee shop and then diverted to the hospital he was been updated by Amy's medical team and told she had already delivered, and with her baby, was on her way by ambulance to the closest hospital. Amy and Elisa (named in honor of Amy's mother, Ellen) were admitted for only one night to make sure they were both healthy enough to go home. Kevin got to the hospital shortly after Amy arrived with their newborn little girl and was conflicted about not being able to help because he was not at the planned meeting with Peter, Amy, and Brian, but was ecstatic that all had turned out to be fine with no complications for Amy for their new family addition.

Now, six weeks after baby Elisa Brady came into the world in that little coffee shop in New York, and four weeks after Heather and Brian were married, a party was underway and in full swing at Kevin's and Amy's home where they were hosting Jake, Alex, the owner of the coffee shop and all of the servers that could make it to this major thank you event.

Back at the party:

"Peter," Brian began, "If it's okay with you, I would appreciate a few minutes alone to talk to you privately. There's a bedroom down the hall where we can talk."

"Absolutely, Brian, let's go. I just need to say goodnight to everyone first, then I'll meet you."

When Peter entered the room where Brian was waiting, Brian looked up from where he was sitting and began delivering what was on his mind.

"Peter, you have no idea how happy I am that you could be here tonight. I'm so glad you reached out to me, and that we're together as a family, and while our parents could not be here this evening, they would be very happy we've found each other and are in each other's lives now. And, Heather and I are thrilled you were able to be at our wedding, cementing our relationship as we head into the future.

I also believe, wherever they are, mom and dad have been watching over us and will also keep Amy, Elisa, Kevin and Heather safe too. So, this is just the beginning of a new relationship between you and the rest of the family, and I need you to know that."

Peter listened intently to Brian carefully deliver his message. He then hugged Brian, and with his eyes now filling with tears of joy.

"Brian, I was unsure at first whether to try to track my biological family down, but now all doubts are gone. I also couldn't ask for a better welcome to the Miller family than what I've experienced since you, Heather, Amy, and Brian have welcomed me into the family. Elisa, of course, is a bonus!"

Brian wiped his eyes and shook hands with Peter.

"Thank you for saying all that, Peter. It's time to say goodnight, but not goodbye. We must stay in touch and get together soon, perhaps at our home in Courtland."

"I agree, Brian. I need to get going. We will stay in touch!"

After Peter left, Brian remained in the bedroom alone for a few minutes to reflect.

Brian left the bedroom and walked outside to a picnic table in Kevin's and Amy's backyard, followed by Flash, to get some air and to reflect even more. He chose to lie down on his back in the soft, tall grass, which had some dew on it, enjoying the cool, crisp breeze coming up the valley while he stared at the dark, black sky.

"Look," Brian told Flash, "There goes a shooting star!"

Flash barked once, then twice more as if he too could see the stars and understood what Brian was saying.

Heather had just walked out into the backyard and caught everything that was happening on her cell phone camera with Brian and Flash on the ground staring at the night sky. Brian then looked up and saw Heather.

Smiling, he asked, "How long have you been standing there?"

With a huge smile on her face, Heater replied, "Long enough, only this time I am the one who captured the great photo that I wanted!"

"How'd you know we were out here?" Brian asked.

"I just followed the footprints in the wet grass. Kevin apparently has not had it cut in a very long time," laughed Heather. "Come back inside, we're cutting cake and getting ice cream."

Brian looked up at Heather.

"Go back inside, we'll be right behind you."

Heather went back into the house as Brian had suggested, knowing he still had a ton of things on his mind, and she could sense it.

Brian continued staring at the sky, mindful that this would be his mother's 60th birthday if she were still alive. Flash snuggled next to Brian, both still on the grass.

Brian looked over at Flash and asked, "Did I ever tell you that when I was in college, I thought I wanted to be a journalist?"

Flash tilted his head to one side, with his ears perked up.

"Yeah, that's true. Oh, don't misunderstand me, Flash, I am not sorry I became a photographer; I am very pleased and proud of my work. In fact, I've received invitations from several schools in the area to teach advanced photography. I have even been invited to speak at some very prestigious conferences about my work. Yep. I have my entire life ahead of me and need to determine what I want to do with the rest of it."

Then Brian and Flash got up and slowly walked back toward the house to join everyone inside, where there was laughter and everyone was cooing over baby Elisa Brady.

Just before he opened the door to enter the house, Brian looked up in time to see another shooting star streaking across the cloudless black sky.

"Maybe someday either I or someone else will write about my life," Brian told Flash.

"Yeah, maybe I should have been a journalist and learned how to write so I could write a story about my life."

Flash barked once and licked Brian's hand as they both headed into the house.

As he went through the door, Brian uttered under his breath to no one in particular, "I wonder what's next?"

About the Author

Jerry R. Rosen is a storyteller and real estate expert who has spent more than 50 years working in housing across the U.S. He built a strong career by improving apartment communities, but his true passion has always been people, relationships, and the strength it takes to keep going.

Jerry grew up in a suburb of Cleveland, Ohio. His life includes quiet moments and big changes – from facing deep personal loss to finding beauty in unexpected places. He now lives in Florida, where he writes, gives advice, and travels.

He often carries his camera, staying curious about the world around him. His first book, *Cut the tape early!*, shares stories from both his work and personal life. His second book, Photos, Footprints and Flash, dives even deeper. It mixes real and imagined stories about loss, healing, and finding strength to begin again.

www.ingramcontent.com/pod-product-compliance
Lightning Source LLC
Chambersburg PA
CBHW071138130626
46553CB00004B/1431